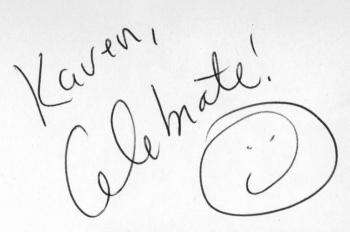

Karen,
Celebrate!

REAL SOLUTIONS
for Ordering Your Private Life

Lori Salierno

REAL SOLUTIONS
for Ordering Your Private Life

Lori Salierno

SERVANT PUBLICATIONS
ANN ARBOR, MICHIGAN

Vine Books is an imprint of Servant Publications especially designed to
serve evangelical Christians.

Published by Servant Publications
P.O. Box 8617
Ann Arbor, Michigan 48107

Cover design by David Uttley Design, Sisters, Oregon

01 02 03 04 10 9 8 7 6 5 4 3 2 1

Printed in the United States of America
ISBN 1-56955-271-1

Library of Congress Cataloging-in-Publication Data

Salierno, Lori.
    Real solutions for ordering your private life / Lori Salierno.
        p. cm.
    ISBN 1-56955-271-1 (alk. paper)
     1. Christian life. 2. Spiritual life. 3. Life skills. I. Title.
    BV4501.3. S25 2001
    248.4—dc21

                                                        2001002867

Contents

Acknowledgments

My heartfelt thanks go to Kay Strom for her skillful assistance from beginning to end. She researched, wrote, edited, and helped me meet all my deadlines. Kay, I am especially grateful to you.

I also want to thank the others who helped and supported me through this project, as well as everyone who has had an influence on my life and has helped me understand the value of a balanced life.

Preface

Our lives resemble a conveyor belt that provides us with an endless supply of choices each day. Depending on our circumstances, the conveyor belt may go faster and faster, until it is out of control, or it may go more slowly. Regardless of the speed, it doesn't seem to stop. It seems to be in constant motion, loudly demanding our attention.

Several years ago, as my life got busier and busier, I began looking at my schedule and realizing how much of my life was driven by that schedule. I loved what I was doing, but this feeling of being out of control did not seem right. What was worse was the fact that everyone around me seemed to be out of control, too, and we would affirm each other for having such busy lives. At times we were even competitive with it, trying to see who was the busiest, whose conveyor belt was going the fastest. Finally, I realized that this was not the way God designed us to live.

Yet, it seemed that when I got one area of my life under control, another area went out of control. I wondered how to achieve balance. I came to the realization that I would have to order my heart before I could order my schedule.

My path to gaining a well-ordered heart led me to a greater challenge. The challenge was not about having the blocks in my calendar filled with the right information, but about the priorities in my life—how they would determine how I would spend my time.

My priorities, although nicely laid out in my schedule, were dictated by people and circumstances. My supply of choices was someone else's and not my own. I determined to make a conscious effort to listen to God about my life and priorities. I became more selective in what I agreed to do. When I began to be more selective, it was not easy on the people who were used to having my time and attention, who now had to find help from another source. Yet I realized that I could not "die on every cross," as my mother used to say.

With time, I did attain a sense of peace and balance. Although my life is far from perfect, I can now detect warning signs when it is time to reflect, regroup, and refocus.

My quest for balance has enabled me to celebrate the moments of each day and to live life fully, with enthusiasm and gusto. In this book, I want to share some of my discoveries in this quest. I want you to be able to enjoy life, not just endure it. This book will give you some practical tips on how to nurture a well-ordered heart, regardless of your station in life, and a well-ordered heart will result in a balanced lifestyle. These tools and tips are meant to be applied, so you, too, can begin to live life with peace, joy, and a great deal of delight. Life is an adventure to be enjoyed, not a conveyor belt to be managed!

Chapter 1

The Race Is On

When I was in the ninth grade, I joined the Shumway Junior High track team. I was a "miler." In my first race I competed against runners from three other schools. We approached the starting line and took our positions. The starter lifted his pistol high and called out: "On your mark! Get set!" Then ...

Pop-pop!

"Shumway runner jumped the gun!" he shouted. "Let's start again!" Again he lifted the starting pistol into the air. "On your mark! Get set!" Then ...

Pop-pop!

"Shumway runner!"

"Yes, sir?" I said.

"Do you know how many laps you have to go when you run the mile?"

"Yes, sir," I answered. "Four laps."

"That's right, you have four laps to run. So there's no need to jump the gun. Why are you jumping the gun?"

I proudly called out my answer: "Because I want to win, sir!"

"Shumway runner," he said, "how you start the race is not

11

what's important. What's important is how you finish it."

This was true for a junior-high miler, but it's even truer in the Christian life. How we start the race is nowhere near as important as how we finish it. Anyone can have an enthusiastic beginning, but few are the people who can go the distance. To do that requires running a balanced race. It is not good enough to pour our all into one area of life and to neglect the others. No, to run the race successfully, we need to be able to weather disappointments, discouragements, and setbacks and still stay on track.

In 2 Corinthians 4, the apostle Paul addresses the church at Corinth and encourages them to go the distance. In these eighteen verses he gives them much important information, including this basic principle of staying power: *Remember who you are.*

In 2 Corinthians 3:17-18, Paul says: "Now the Lord is the Spirit, and where the Spirit of the Lord is, there is freedom. And we, who with unveiled faces all reflect the Lord's glory, are being transformed into His likeness with ever increasing glory, which comes from the Lord, who is the Spirit."

The very first thing Paul does in these verses is to remind the Corinthian Christians who they are! They are people with unveiled faces. They are unique and different. God loves them, and He makes them very special.

You can never hope to achieve true balance in your personal life unless you begin to see yourself through God's eyes. When you are hit with a barrage of negative criticism, tricked by lies, or shaken by circumstances, only His perspective of you will keep you on an even keel. So, here they are, straight from the Source—positive truths about you. Any time you're feeling down, doubtful, or discouraged, repeat these verses to yourself.

- I have peace with God (Romans 5:1)
- I am accepted by God (Ephesians 1)
- I am a child of God (John 1:12)
- I am filled by the Holy Spirit (1 Corinthians 2:12)
- I have access to God's wisdom (James 1:5)
- I am helped by God (Hebrews 4:16)
- I am reconciled to God (Romans 5:11)
- I have no condemnation (Romans 8:1)
- I am justified (Romans 5:1)
- I have God's righteousness (2 Corinthians 5:21 and Romans 5:19)
- I am God's representative (2 Corinthians 5:20)
- I am completely forgiven (Colossians 1:14)
- I am sustained by God (Philippians 4:19)
- I am tenderly loved (Jeremiah 31:3)
- I am the aroma of Christ to God (2 Corinthians 2:15)
- I am a temple of God (1 Corinthians 3:16)
- I am blameless and beyond reproach (Colossians 1:22)

We are God's people, unique and special. Let us never forget our significance.

God created you to be the very best you can be. Experience the freedom of being that person. Appreciate your uniqueness. Experience God's love and truly enjoy who you are.

If you can come to see yourself this way, you won't have to prove your worth to anyone, including yourself. When you fail, this truth will give you the energy and the courage to dust yourself off and start over again.

> *Your value and identity do come not from what you do, but from who you are in Christ.*

Christian, if you are going to go the distance, begin with an understanding of who you are, and never forget it.

What Is a Balanced Life?

The president of the printing company where Charlie works shares the year's profits by giving Christmas bonuses. Charlie is an industrious worker. He comes in early and stays until the job is done, however late that may be. When he opens his bonus envelope and sees the check for $500 he is thrilled. With the cost of the car repair and the leaking water heater, he can certainly use that money. But when he realizes that everyone else got the same amount he did, his pleasure quickly fades. No one works as hard as he does. "If I had more time, I'd start my own business," Charlie says for the hundredth time. "Then I could reap the rewards of my efforts and long hours. If I only had the time...."

* * *

Paula's aerobics class has ended, and she is pooped. "Hi!" a classmate calls out to her. "Want to come downstairs for a quick game of racquetball?" Paula musters every bit of energy she has left to smile and say, "Not today, thanks." She would be in better shape if she came to the gym on a more regular basis. Yet how can she? Her kids and job take every moment of the day.

* * *

Sunday dinner at Mom and Dad's house. Monday night football. Tuesday computer class. Wednesday with the kids. Thursday, Friday, Saturday—every day is spoken for. You'd love to get involved in a Bible study, but right now your schedule is just too tight.

* * *

What is a balanced life, anyway? Is it merely a question of finding time to move to a more satisfying business, to improve your health, or to study God's Word? Is it setting goals to be accomplished just as soon as the kids finish school, the wedding is over, you pay for that great summer vacation, or the holidays are past? Is it putting your life on hold until some future, more quiet time?

Well, I can tell you right now what a balanced life is *not*. It is not merely a matter of having more time. You have twenty-four hours in a day right now, and that is all you will ever have. None of us is given the gift of more time. Neither is a balanced life a perfect life. As long as we live in this world, that is something that is out of reach. Finally, a balanced life is not a life that is permanently *set*. No, a balanced life is always fluctuating.

OK, you may be saying, *so what* is *a balanced life*?

First of all, a balanced life is a life that is ordered by the Spirit of God, one in which His Spirit has transformed the heart by grace. From this foundation comes the strength and wisdom to live a life in which all facets honor God. A balanced life, then, is a life that is driven by priorities and perspectives centered on Christ.

Your life is not a pie, to be cut into equal pieces and conscientiously dished out to your job, your family, your church, and so forth. Rather, balance starts at the center and reaches out into the spiritual, physical, emotional, mental, and relational aspects of your life. The key to a balanced life is to find that center.

Is Balance Really All That Important?

To get an idea of its importance, compare imbalance in your life to the ride you get in a car with tires that are out of balance. Can you get where you're going? Yes. But on the way the ride will be bumpy and uncomfortable. It will cause you stress and pain. And there is always the chance that the imbalance will cause a major setback in your trip.

Yet, if you get there anyway, why is balance so terribly important? Because people who lack a sense of balance in their lives lose so very much. Some lose their walk with

God. Some lose their families. Some lose their jobs. Some lose their sanity. Almost all lose their joy.

Well, that's not me, you may be saying. *I mean, sure, I do spend too much time at work, and I don't get any exercise, but other than that, my life is pretty well-balanced.*

Pretty well-balanced? That means you have work to do. For, you see, if any one area gets out of balance, it automatically impacts and handicaps the others. A lack of balance in one area means a lack of balance everywhere.

Back in the 1800s, there were slaves who, though freed by the Emancipation Proclamation, still chose to live in slavery. Why? Because for them freedom was a frightening unknown.

They were not alone in this. Consider the Israelites who were freed from their slavery in Egypt. Very soon they were longing for the leeks, garlic, and cucumbers they ate in captivity. They were willing to go back to Egypt and become slaves again just to satisfy their appetites!

This is one of the great dangers of imbalance. Once we get used to it, it seems comfortable enough to us. We put up with the bumpy road, or the pain and stress the ride causes, because it's all we know. We assume that this is as good as it gets. We adjust to a life out of balance, and we excuse the discomforts, setbacks, and even the enslavement it causes us.

Why Are Our Lives So Out of Balance?

In our society we are evaluated by our performance rather than by the quality of our "being." So, to placate those around us, we do what we think will satisfy and impress them, and, because we cannot do everything, we put aside those things that others don't consider to be all that important.

> *Imbalance comes from the notion that what we do determines who we are. In reality, who we are determines the effectiveness of what we do.*

Practically everyone, it seems, complains about not having enough time. No wonder there are so many recent books out on the subject of time management. People insist:

- "I feel guilty if I take time for myself. It seems so selfish."
- "It does me no good to set down goals. I just don't have the self-discipline to stick to them."
- "I don't know what's missing in my life, but I know something is."
- "I know I spend a lot of time at work, but if I don't I'm afraid my income will drop. We couldn't manage on any less."
- "The problem with church is that it takes up too much time. Once you start going, they want you to become involved. I just don't have time to do that."

Is it any wonder that our lives are so out of balance?

Balance Is Driven by Priorities and Perspective

Balance, you see, is much more than simple time management.

Balance in your personal life is determined not so much by *how* you spend your time, but by whether or not you let your priorities make that determination.

Although this sounds easy enough, far too many people don't practice it. In fact, it has been suggested that the very worst mistake people make in time management is that they spend their time on concerns that are not their true priorities.

Think of it this way: in each day of your life there are *debits* and there are *credits*. When you subtract the debits and add the credits, does your day end up in balance? How about your week? Your month? Your year?

Here's an example to give you an idea of how this works:

Debits

- Your child forgot his lunch and you had to run it over to him. (subtract 20 minutes)
- Your phone rang four times during dinner, each time interrupting your family's sharing time. (subtract 12 minutes)
- On your credit card bill, the charge for a car rental was double-billed. You had to straighten it out. (subtract 20 minutes)
- There was a storm and the lights went out. The batteries in the flashlight didn't work and you had to search for candles and matches. (subtract 30 minutes)

- You brought work home from the office. Without some of the support information, it took you longer than expected to get it done. (subtract 2 hours)

Credits
- You started the day by reading a Psalm and asking God to bless your day. (add 15 minutes)
- A friend invited you to join a book club. You are already into the first book and are enjoying it thoroughly. (add 1 hour)
- You left work early so you could get to your daughter's soccer game on time. (add 30 minutes)
- In an exchange of services, you did accounting work for a housecleaning firm and they cleaned your house. (add 2 hours)

In this example, the sum of the debits is 3 hours and 22 minutes. The sum of the credits is 3 hours and 45 minutes. This is a pretty good balance, especially since it is 23 minutes ahead on credits!

As you look over the debits in the example, you may say, *"Hold it! Why is that a debit? It wasn't a bad thing to do."* No, maybe not *bad*. But could it have been *better*? Could it have been *best*? Take the first item on the list. Is it bad to take your child's lunch to school for him? Certainly not. But would it have been better to have him buy a school lunch and take the forgotten one the following day? Not only would this save you time, but it might also help him develop responsibility and independence. Now consider the book club that earned a one-hour credit. For some people that might be a completely positive use of time, but for others it might be just one more thing to have to get done. In that case, it would actually be a debit.

The point is to apply this to your own life, and to balance what is good against what is better, and then to balance that against what is best. It's a lot like balancing a checking account. If every day you take out more money than you put in, in time you will run out, whether you start with one dollar or one million dollars. The same is true with the hours in your day.

If you are like most people in our society, you will find that television, videos, and the Internet account for a big chunk of your time. Is that a debit or a credit? According to a study by Leisure Trends between 1990 and 1992 and reported in *American Demographics* magazine, Americans spend 30 percent of their free time in front of the television set. If you were tightening up your budget, what would you do? Trim the nonessentials! It's the same with balancing your time. Since television viewing is a major time drain, if you want to make the best use of your time, you have several options:

1. **Go ahead and enjoy watching television**. For some people, it is quite relaxing. Instead of feeling guilty, set yourself a sensible time limit, then give yourself permission to sit back and enjoy it. But be disciplined. Don't allow yourself to go over your time limit.

2. **Double up**. Do something else while you are watching: ride a stationary bike, write letters, sew on buttons, file papers, fold laundry.

3. **Be selective**. Videotape your favorite shows and specials and watch them at your convenience, fast-forwarding through the commercials. This will keep you from getting caught up in time-wasting channel surfing.

4. **Pull the plug**. Turn the television off for seven days and see what happens to your schedule. You will probably find that you and your family read more and spend more time talking to one another. It just may happen that you will decide to keep it off permanently.

True Priorities

You cannot trust that your balance will be driven by your own priorities unless you are aware of just what your priorities are. List them below:

1._____

2._____

3._____

4._____

5._____

6._____

OK, we will come back to your list in a minute. First, it's important to note that many people have two priority lists:

- their true priorities
- their "should" priorities

Most are hesitant to admit to themselves or to others what they truly want. Instead, they work on what they believe *should* be their priorities. The problem is, when we hold both false and true priorities, the natural result is stress and confusion. This is hardly the thing to help us achieve balance!

With that in mind, look back over your list and do some evaluation. Did you list only true priorities, or did some "should" priorities slip onto your list? If you suspect so, ask yourself who it is that you want to please. Is it:

- your parents?
- other family members?
- friends and neighbors?
- society?
- people in your church?
- people at work?
- someone else?

Go back over your list and put a check mark beside any items you suspect are "should" priorities rather than true priorities.

Are there some priorities you need to rewrite? If so, take time to do that now.

In the space below, list the three you consider to be your top true priorities:

1. _____

2. _____

3. _____

Congratulations! You now have your priorities set. That's an important step. Yet it's not the final step. How are you going to stick to these priorities? Here is my suggestion, in four steps:

Step #1: Hang your list of priorities somewhere where you cannot help but see it every morning. (The bathroom mirror is a great place.)

Step #2: Read over your list every morning, renewing your commitment to your priorities each time.

Step #3: Ask yourself: "What can I do today that will help me achieve my top priority?"

Step #4: Be sure to do that thing.

Very soon you will see your priorities becoming reality.

From My Heart to Yours

Most of us today run in the fast lane of life. There are many different reasons why we choose this lane. Yet it is here that we absolutely must pause and examine the bulky weight of constant busy-ness that comes with running in the fast lane. The fact is, we are going to have difficulty finishing our race if we continue at the speed at which we are running. If we are going to persevere, then we must learn to run a balanced race. This will require spiritual nourishment; physical, mental, and emotional health; and balance in our various relationships, from family to church to work, and everywhere in between. Busy-ness must be countered with rest, comfort, and refreshment.

Please understand right here, at the beginning, that I am speaking to you as one who is still learning. Like you, I continue to struggle to find the best balance in my own life. Yet I also speak to you out of the depth of my experience—what I have learned from others and what I have learned from the hard knocks I've suffered in family life and in serving the Lord in ministry. Let me share with you my two rock-bottom reminders and my three basic axioms for achieving balance in life.

First, the reminders:

Rock-Bottom Reminder #1: The One Good Thing Rule

This is a great thing to make a part of your daily life: Every day, in every area of your life, find the one good thing.

One time when my husband Kurt and I were youth leaders, we were on a bus bringing a group of kids back home to Phoenix from Los Angeles. Wouldn't you know it, our bus broke down in the middle of the desert! The kids were baking in the summertime heat, with no air conditioning. We had started out on this trip with so much enthusiasm, but now here we were and there was not a scrap of that enthusiasm left. The kids were irritated with us, angry at the situation, and increasingly bickering with each other. My husband was frustrated and growing more upset by the minute. The whole situation was completely negative.

Now, I don't like negative thinking. So, while my husband was outside in the blazing heat, trying to fix the engine, I stood up in the bus and said, "Guys, I just want to say something to you. Negative thinking drains us of our spiritual power. It drains us of creative well-being. So here's what we're going to do. We're going to find the one good thing in this situation. Yes, right now. Each one of you is to think of one good thing about being stranded in the desert in a broken-down bus."

Needless to say, they weren't very excited about my idea. To say they gave me negative looks is putting it kindly. So I said, "I'm serious here, guys. Every one of you is going to have to come up with one good thing." Then I started down the rows. It was really hard for them to get started, but once they did, it became quite humorous. They said things like:

"Well, at least none of us are hurt."

"We won't get in an accident."

"We're together. We're not out here alone."

"We're learning patience."

"We're not freezing!"

"We'll get a lot of good stories out of this."

By the time my husband got back on the bus, the whole climate had changed. It was still baking hot, but now everyone was laughing and talking. He looked at me in amazement and asked, "What happened to these kids?"

"Simple!" I said. "They found the one good thing."

Those kids had gained a sense of perspective on their situation, and with that perspective came a real sense of balance.

You say you can't find one good thing in your situation? I know it may not be easy to get started. The good thing was not easy to come by in that hot bus, either. But pause a minute. Ask God to show you the redeeming factor right where you are.

Once you find that one good thing, say it out loud. Yes, even if you are all alone. We need to hear ourselves say, "You know what, Lord? I found the one good thing here. It is...."

Rock-Bottom Reminder #2: Each Day, Determine Something for Which to Be Thankful

The companion to reminder #1 is to identify one thing each day that is worthy of your gratitude. Again, speak it out loud: "Dear Lord, today I want to thank you for...."

Each day, in any and every situation, make these two rules an automatic part of your life. Speak aloud those things that are true, honorable, right, pure, lovely, admirable, excellent, or praiseworthy. After all, these are the things about which the apostle Paul tells us to think (see Phil 4:8). When you think about these things, you're going to have a balance to your mentality, a balance emotionally, and a balance in your perspective. That, right there, is a redeeming factor.

Now, the axioms:

Axiom #1: Find the Positive in Each Situation

If you can find the positive in every situation you face, your most negative feelings will be replaced with a sense of joy and laughter that can bring a calmness to a heavy-laden heart, even one that is working through extremely difficult things. You say you doubt that it's possible to see anything positive in your current situation? Don't be so sure. Take a look at the cross of Jesus Christ. As Jesus' followers watched Him suffer that most pathetic, disgusting of deaths, they must have thought, *There can be nothing positive in this!* Yet God knew otherwise. Three days later, He showed them the positive in all its magnificent glory: Jesus Christ, risen from the grave! Jesus Christ, Redeemer of humanity! Jesus Christ, Savior of the world. Talk about finding a positive in a negative situation!

If you are a child of God, you have every reason to think positively. In fact, a positive perspective should be your regular outlook on life.

Axiom #2: Discover One Thing to Laugh About Each Day

Did you know that you will be much more likely to solve a problem if you take time for something fun and delightful before you go on to that problem? You were created for laughter! God Himself created it. He is a God of hope, love, and joy—and, yes, of laughter, too.

We need to let go and not take ourselves so seriously. When Kurt and I moved to Phoenix, I went to a gymnasium. I walked in and these guys were making grunting noises, cussing, hitting each other. Talk about a negative feeling! There sure was one in that gym. I thought, "Lord, we've got to do something here."

I walked over to the bench press, where smelly, sweating guys were chanting, "Be the weight! Be the weight!" Then, as they lifted the weights, they grunted, "Huh! Huh! Hoo! Hoo!"

So I got in there and grabbed a bar that had no weights. I lay back and gave two loud exhales, then chanted, "I gotta be the weight! I gotta be the weight! I gotta be the weight! Ooohaaah! Ooohaaah! Ooohaaah!"

Let me tell you, every guy in the gym stopped and stared at me. Well, I was brand new. I didn't know anybody, so there was no reason to be embarrassed. I wiped my face and exclaimed, "Whew! Oh, hi, men."

One guy walked over and stood in front of me, glowering. "You know what your problem is?" he stated. "Your problem is that you have way too much fun! This place is serious! We don't goof around here! We don't laugh in here! We are serious about sweating; we are serious about developing our bodies!"

I stood up. "You want to know what your problem is?" I asked. Everyone's attention was riveted on me. "This is not a hospital," I continued. "This is not work. It's a gymnasium. Recreation. Fun. Exercise. Joy. You guys come in here and spit and slap and cuss like it's some deathly place. Now, I'm new to the gym" (as if that weren't perfectly obvious). "My goal is to bench my weight. And when I do it, I want there to be whooping and hollering and whistling and clapping and cheering, and I want there to be a celebration. Do I make myself perfectly clear?"

I went back the next day. I sat down and put five on each side. As I did this, one guy came over and said, "Oh, you need to breathe out when you push it up ... but we're having fun! We're having fun!" So I did a couple more. And more the next day, and the next day, and the next. It took me several months, but I kept working. As I worked, some of the guys would go by and say, "Just be the weight. Just be the weight. You breathed out when you pushed up; be the weight." Then they would add, "Guys, we're having fun."

Others would chime in: "We're having fun—be the weight, be the weight." In this way they would help me.

After a year of regular workouts at the gym, I awoke one morning and told my husband, "Kurt, I'm gonna bench-press my weight today."

I walked into the gym. I didn't say anything to the friends I had made; I just picked out my weight and sat down. Suddenly one guy called out, "Whoa! Whoa! Guys! Everyone! I think the mama is gonna do her weight!" Then he looked straight at me and said, "Ma'am, if I'm not mistaken—is this your weight?"

I said, "Maybe."

"Yep, it is! Guys!" he called. So everybody stopped and gathered around.

"Hey, you don't have to do this," I said.

"No, no!" they replied. "We had our orders. We know what to do."

I said meekly, "I have no idea if I can even do it." Yet I lay back and got ready.

"Remember. Breathe out. Be the weight, and get it off your chest," one guy said. "Just give it all you've got. But we're having a good time—having a good time!"

So I got under the weight. (Grunting, panting, groaning.) It was a lot of weight to bench. (More grunting, panting, groaning.) But I made it!

"Wooooh! Wooooh! Woooh! Wooh!" The guys yelled. They slapped each other and shouted, "Good job! Good job!"

Then the first guy came over and said, "Umm ... What makes you so different, lady? Last year this place was nothing but a death trap. Then in walks this chick who tells us we're not allowed to spit, cuss, and yip. That we have to laugh, whoop and holler, slap each other, and high-five. What happened?"

"I'll tell you what happened," I said. "I have a God who has a playful spirit. He's full of joy. He's full of life. He's full of laughter. He's full of hope. It's just the way Christians live, and I shared it with you."

I know that some personalities have a more difficult time laughing than others. I realize some people just don't see things in a very humorous light. Yet, ask the Lord for little moments of humor, and pause from your busy day to laugh. Just watch what lightness and balance will come about!

Axiom #3: Look Forward to One Thing Each Week

Every week, find something to which you can look forward. It might be nothing more than going to the library and reading a good book, or watching a ball game on television. It might be calling up a friend and saying, "Let's go out for coffee." It might be something as great as a big date with your spouse.

One time Kurt picked me up at the airport after a long trip. I was exhausted. He said, "Lori, we have a date night tonight."

I said, "Kurt, no. Not tonight. I'm really too tired."

"Nope," he said. "You're going to go home, take a shower, and put on something nice. Then we're going out."

I knew perfectly well that this was all my fault; I had trained him this way. I had always told him, "Why don't you sometimes think up a date? We'll just do it!" Well, now he'd thought one up and I didn't want to do it. So I sighed and complained as I dressed quickly and not that well. Then I walked out the door and there stood a white limousine. The driver stepped up, opened the door, and said, "Madame, your date has hired me to take the two of you to dinner."

I had never been in a limousine before! I grabbed the driver and gave him a big, big hug, all the time jumping up and down and exclaiming, "Oooooooh!" The driver just shook his head and said, "You don't get out much, do you?"

Well, we got into that limousine and I was all energy. I helped myself to the soda pop they had in there; I turned all the lights on; I opened the sky roof.

"I see you got your energy back," Kurt said.

"Oh, of course I got my energy back!" I said. "Take me out to dinner!"

I told him I didn't care where he took me. Any old hamburger place would be fine. We could just whip out a white tablecloth and a candle and it would be great. People would walk in, look at us, and say, "Oh, isn't that ... uh ... different?" and I would tell them, "It's the thing I looked forward to all week!"

Most of my one-thing-per-weeks are not as magnificent as a limo ride, but whether big or small, I eagerly look forward to each of them.

The choices we make every hour of every day create our future.

Balance Journal

Reading is fine, but to get the greatest benefit, it is important to process the information you read and then to make it your own. To help you do this, at the end of each chapter I will make suggestions for things you might want to jot down in a Balance Journal. I suggest you get a notebook and keep it just for this purpose.

Here is the Balance Journal assignment for this chapter:

- In your journal, list the priorities in your life. Now rate each one from 1 to 10 (10 being the most trivial and 1 the most important).

- Look at your top three priorities. What are some actions you can take to help you achieve them?

Keep your Balance Journal with you as you go through this book. You will likely think of other things you will want to jot down in it. Before you go on to each new chapter, it will be good to review what you have written.

Now we will begin the balancing act with Spiritual Balance.

Chapter 2

Spiritual Balance

For a day in Thy courts is better than
A thousand outside.
I would rather stand at the threshold
Of the house of my God,
Than dwell in the tents of wickedness.

PSALM 84:10 NASB

Is there anything that draws us into spiritual balance more than the Psalms? I don't think so. Within them we see praise and adoration like nowhere else. We also see lament and fear, discouragement and doubt. Yet through it all, David, the greatest of the psalmists, triumphantly states that if he had his choice between one single day in God's presence or a thousand among those who do not honor God, it would be no contest at all. The one day in God's presence would win, hands down. Now, that is spiritual balance!

A Sense of God's Spirit

Can we ever hope to maintain a sense of God's Spirit in this chaotic, unpredictable world? Only if we make a definite, concentrated effort to do so. It won't just happen, that's for sure. If we rely on external structures to provide continuity and security in our day-to-day living, we're going to be in trouble, because the external structures of our lives often go through complete changes. Therefore, we must have the inner strength to handle whatever circumstances or external structures may alter in our lives.

"But," some people insist, "I sense God's Spirit in me by the ways in which He uses me."

This is great, but there is one very important thing we must understand: God works *in* us before He works *through* us.

It can't happen through you if it hasn't happened to you.
—Lloyd John Ogilvie

Spiritual balance means yielding ourselves completely to God and resting in Him. To help you do this, consider Psalm 91. This psalm is a glowing testimony to the security of those who put their trust in the provision and safety of God. Verses 1 and 2 tell us:

He who dwells in the shelter of the
   Most High
will rest in the shadow of the Almighty.
I will say of the Lord, "He is my
   refuge and my fortress,
my God, in whom I trust."

Do you want a sense of God's Spirit? Then dwell in the shadow of the Most High. Rest in His presence. Claim Him as your refuge and your fortress. Ahhh, now that is real peace.

Yet, this is not easy to do in our culture. We are in such a mode of producing and doing that we have forgotten the importance of *being*. The fact is, however, our *being* must precede our *doing*. Only then will we have the maturity to lean back and receive God's best from His merciful hands.

The unweaned child is at its mother's breast for what it wants—milk. The weaned child, however, is content to rest in its loving mother's arms and receive whatever she desires to give.

—M. Robert Mulholland Jr.
Invitation to a Journey
(interpretation of Psalm 131:2)

Whenever Jesus went through Bethany, He stopped to see His good friends Mary and Martha. They were always happy to see their Lord. One day when He arrived Mary rushed to sit at His feet, eager to listen to all that He had to say. Martha knew that He would be spending the night, so she rushed around to make everything perfect for His stay. And of course there was dinner to make. Finally, as she paused to wipe her face and brush the hair out of her eyes, a thought occurred to her: How come she was doing all the work while her sister was sitting and enjoying their company? She stomped into the front room and announced, "Lord, don't you care that my sister has left me to do everything by myself? Tell her to help me!"

"Martha, Martha," Jesus answered patiently. "You are worried and upset about so many things, but only one thing is really important. Mary has chosen what is better, and it will not be taken away from her."

Hmmm. That tells us something, doesn't it? If we are not careful, we, like Martha, can allow constant busy-ness to crowd out the gold and silver that could have been part of our lives. If we are to run the race well, we absolutely must make it a priority to withdraw and replenish ourselves spiritually, emotionally, and physically. We cannot allow our busy-ness to get us so out of balance that we fall down exhausted at the end of the race—or perhaps before it is even over. Sure, there is a great deal that has to be done in this life. Yet God wants us to do all that we do in His name and to His glory. The only way we can do that is to come to Him regularly for the spiritual rest, refreshment, and guidance we need to run our race well.

The times I've overworked and made myself and everyone else miserable, it's been because I needed people's appreciation, or their pity, or their admiration too much. I was trying to prove I was worth something by my hard work.... But when service becomes a pain, or a means of personal gain, then the service needs to be curtailed for the sake of the higher good of resting in Christ's presence. God called you to be His beloved, not His beast of burden.

—Frank Barker
"The Martha Syndrome"

How can we gain the inner strength we need to run the race well? The only way I know is to spend time with God each day. Before you start listing all the reasons why this just won't work for you, let me hasten to say that I understand that a person's particular station in life may require that he or she use some creativity in developing spiritual disciplines. Certainly a spiritually balanced life looks different for each of these individuals:

- The mother of infant twins
- The parent of a rebellious teenager
- A busy student
- A retired person
- A single person
- Someone staggering in the wake of a tragedy
- The CEO of a large corporation
- A Christian living in a family of nonbelievers

Time with the Lord, sitting at His feet in worship, doesn't need to take a specific amount of time. It doesn't have to happen at a particular hour or place, and it need not have a distinct format.

Let me tell you about Colin, the seven-year-old son of friends of ours. He and his mom were riding with my husband Kurt and me one afternoon. Kurt and Colin's mom were having a deep discussion, and Colin was looking at me with an engrossed look.

"Colin," I said, "what are you thinking?"

"Miss Lori," Colin said, "I was just wondering, do you ever have two-second conversations with God?"

"Two-second conversations with God?" I asked. "What do you mean, Colin?"

"Well, sometimes, all of a sudden, I have a two-second conversation where God just speaks to me and then, Boom! He's gone. It's like just in a moment," Colin said. "I can hear His voice, and I can tell He's right here. And I just wondered, does that ever happen to you? Do you have two-second conversations with God?"

I looked at that little boy and I realized that God's Spirit was speaking to him. "Colin," I said, "do you know what? I used to have those two-second conversations with God, just like you. And I, too, would sense His presence intensely."

Colin looked straight at me and said, "How come you don't anymore?"

"Well, I guess I'm too busy doing other things, like writing talks and meeting with people and writing papers for my doctorate," I explained lamely. Then, after a moment,

I added, "I'm afraid I'm so busy, and I've cluttered up my life so much, that I can't hear those two-second conversations anymore."

Colin was perplexed. "Miss Lori," he asked, "why would you want to write a paper or talk to people when you can hear God for two seconds?" I was silent, but Colin continued to press. "Why do you think I can still hear Him, but you can't?"

"Colin," I said, "it's because you're fresh from God. And you don't have things in your life that clutter it up. You have the ability to sense God's presence in the simple moments of life. I've crowded those things out."

After that conversation, I took the matter to God in my prayer time. I repented for no longer having those moments of intense awareness of His presence. I thanked Him for allowing a little seven-year-old boy to remind me that those moments are more precious than anything I can ever do or encounter.

I truly believe that it is in seeing the humor in life, and in rediscovering simple pleasures, that we discover why we were created. We can be in Christ, and be aware of His presence, even in the midst of all the different things going on in our lives, if we just train our senses to become aware of Him.

The fruit of prayer is a deepening of faith.
And the fruit of faith is love,
and the fruit of love is service.
But to be able to pray we need silence,
silence of the heart.
The soul needs time to go away and pray,
to use the mouth,
to use the eyes,
to use the whole body,
and if we don't have that silence,
then we don't know how to pray.

—Mother Theresa
Words to Love By

Solitude, Silence, and Spiritual Rest

Some of the lessons we learn in life come wrapped in emotions, situations, and choices that are extremely difficult to endure. In fact, many people believe spiritual insight can come only through difficult lessons, painful realizations, and heartbreaking sacrifices. Yet these people are wrong. Not all life's lessons come through hard times. Some come to us through joy and rest and answered prayer.

Spiritual Rest

We all know how vital physical rest is to the body. Even more important to our balanced well-being, however, is spiritual rest. Why is it, then, that so many of us miss out on it? This is especially perplexing when we realize how many of us long for it in the deepest part of our beings. Spiritual rest from God includes Sabbath rest, in which we take a break and rest from our work just as God rested from His.

In Philippians 4:6-7 the apostle Paul writes: "Do not be anxious about anything, but in everything, by prayer and petition, with thanksgiving, present your requests to God. And the peace of God, which transcends all understanding, will guard your hearts and minds in Christ Jesus."

This is the essence of spiritual rest.

We need rest from our guilt, doubt, confusion, emptiness, dryness, and despair. We long for the peace of God that transcends all understanding.

—Dr. Siang-Yang Tan
Rest

Solitude and Silence

We all know what silence is, but what exactly is the solitude for which we are searching? Simply put, it is spending time alone with God. To seek solitude is to deliberately withdraw from all human contact or interaction for the sole purpose of meeting with our Lord. Is it hard? You bet it is. Most of us are surrounded by people and noise and jobs that need to be done ASAP. Yet, solitude is an important spiritual discipline. If cultivated and nurtured, it yields a great bounty. It frees us from things, from the opinions of people, from the values and evaluations of those around us. We can begin to truly trust and rely on the Lord. In the quiet and solitude, we can learn to meet with Him in a whole new way.

Without solitude it is virtually impossible to live a spiritual life.

—Henri Nouwen
Making All Things New

How might you spend a time of solitude? Here is a suggestion: Take a silent prayer sabbatical. Because it is so vital to focus on praying, I'd like to suggest prayer days and prayer retreats, times when you get away for four to six hours to be alone and pray. You may be able to get away for a day and a night, or maybe for two days or even an entire weekend. Spend part of the time praising God, waiting before Him, confessing your sins, and reading God's Word, but most of all spend the time in prayer. Take walks. Sit in the sun. Sit on the grass under the shade of a tree. The point is to be alone with the Lord. I am big on studying the Scriptures and memorizing God's Word, but this is not the time or place for these endeavors. This is the time to listen. E. Stanley Jones had what he called his "listening post," a certain fence post where he would go to simply stand and listen. Unless we designate a place and time to listen, we are sure to spend most of our time talking or doing.

Just stand and listen? you may be asking. *Listen to what?*

To God. I suggest you ask directly: "Lord, what are you saying to me?" You see, God is constantly speaking to us. The question is not whether there is anything to listen to. It is whether we are actively listening and in tune to what He is saying.

Here is where silence and solitude come in. Listening takes place during these times. It happens in quietness, when we are separated from the things that would otherwise take our attention. Granted, we can have moments of solitude in the midst of our hectic schedules, but there should be a place and a time for us to simply withdraw. Jesus is our ultimate example, and that is exactly what He did. Take a fair amount of time, be silent before God, and ask Him, "Lord, what are you saying to me?"

A man once approached Mother Teresa and said, "I don't sense God's presence in my life."

"There are two things you can do that will bring God's presence back to your life," she told him. "Number one, spend an hour a day praising His character, just praising who and what God is. Number two, stop doing what displeases Him." Then she looked straight at the man and said, "If you will do those two things over a period of time— stop doing what you know displeases God, and spend an hour a day adoring His character—His presence will return to you in fullness, through Jesus Christ."

I firmly believe that sometimes we need to do exactly this. There are things we are intentionally doing that block God's grace and presence in our lives. Spending time adoring Him will help to correct that imbalance.

When we go into solitude, our primary motivation should not be to plead with God for help. Too many of our prayers run this way: "God, help me. God, do this for me. God, do that for my friend or my family." There is nothing wrong with presenting our petitions to our Heavenly Father. We are commanded to do so. Yet, our times of solitude should be spent listening and loving. This will bring the balance that is so sorely missing in our lives—and, I might add, in our society and our churches as well!

Truly I have set my soul in silence and in peace,
like a weaned child at its mother's breast.

PSALM 131:2

Practicing Solitude and Silence

Here are some guidelines to help you as you get started practicing solitude and silence:

- Schedule times to be alone with the Lord each day. (Don't worry about the length of that scheduled time right now. It is far better to plan for ten minutes and really do it than to set the lofty goal of one hour and be sporadic about it.)

- Periodically set aside an hour for silence, then try to work up to two hours.
- Listen to God more than you speak to Him. (This works well with other people, too, by the way!)
- Begin planning for a daylong retreat where you can be alone with God in solitude and silence.

A quiet time is a time set aside to deepen your knowledge of the Lord, to enrich your own personal relationship with Him, to fellowship with Him, to love Him, to worship Him, on a very personal basis.

—Shirley Rice
The Christian Home: A Woman's View

Christian Fellowship

Christian fellowship means gathering together with other believers for the purpose of worshipping God. This may be in a church congregation or it may be in a small group, such as a home Bible study. Taken a step farther, it also includes serving and caring for one another, praying and reading Scripture together, and reaching out to the world in the love of Christ.

The Christian life should be filled with joy and celebration, but for too many it is more of a chore, or a guilty feeling because it seems as though nothing is being accomplished. Why is this so? One big reason is that we try to do everything alone: we pray alone, we read the Bible alone, we carry our own burdens, and we reach out a helping hand all by ourselves. We live our Christian lives independently rather than linked together with other believers. This means we cannot easily share one another's joys and successes, nor can we adequately comfort others in their sorrow and pain. We don't experience the support that real Christian fellowship should bring, and we are unable to use our spiritual gifts as God intends us to use them.

True Christian fellowship not only allows us to be there for others who need us, but also draws out a willingness in us to ask for and to receive help when we need it. It also calls us to be more honest, transparent, and vulnerable with one another.

Realize Your Ministry

Each of us has a ministry. God has chosen us to accomplish His mission in this world. We are His agents here, His method of operating. We are His vessels. In 2 Corinthians 5:18 we read: "All this is from God, who reconciled us to Himself through Christ and gave us the ministry of reconciliation." Did you get that? God has literally entrusted us with the message of reconciliation! We are ambassadors, allowing God to make His appeal through us. What an awesome privilege!

Yet, this means we must be good stewards of this privilege, for it is also a responsibility. We must not give up. We must not lose heart.

> Without us, He will not; and without Him, we cannot.

A few years ago, when I visited the country of Jordan, I went to see the ancient site of Petra. In order to get to the rock fortress, we had to go by horseback along a trail lined with 750-feet-high rock walls. Each person on that tour had a horse and a personal Arabian guide. I leaned forward on my horse and said to my guide, "Sir, my name is Lori. What is yours?"

"Mohammed," he answered.

I said, "Mohammed, do you know that Jesus Christ loves you? And do you know that He died on the cross for you?" I made a cross with my fingers.

Mohammed looked up at me and said, "Sorry, no speak English."

I prayed, *God, I do not speak his language, and he does not speak my language. How can I communicate Your love to him?"* And in a still, small voice, God said, "Sing him a song."

"Mohammed," I said, "I'm going to teach you a song."

"No, Lori!" he exclaimed. "No, no, no, no!"

I didn't pay any attention to his objections. I leaned up on the horse and said, "It goes like this...." Then I sang,

God is so good.

God is so good.

God is so good,

He's so good to me.

"Now, Mohammed," I said, "I want you to repeat after me."

He said, "No sing, Lori. Please, no sing!"

"Mohammed," I said, "you can either sing it with me or I'll sing it louder."

"OK, OK. Shhhhh! Don't sing it louder! I sing, I sing!"

So we sang through the song, with me singing a line and Mohammed, slowly and very off-key, copying it. After each line I enthusiastically exclaimed, "That's great, Mohammed! That's just great!"

When we finished, Mohammed said, "Lori, let us sing together!" I agreed, and with a loud voice (and still off-key) he sang, "God is so good ..." and because we were between the two cliffs, his voice echoed, "Good, good, good, good."

His friends, who were leading the other people, looked at me accusingly and insisted, "What are you doing to our friend?"

Yet Mohammed kept right on singing: "God is so good (good, good, good, good)," over and over again, accompanied by my warning, "Mohammed, shhhhh! Not so loud!"

Finally, we got to the rock fortress, and Mohammed said to me, "Lori, bring all your friends around. I want to sing them a song."

"Come here, you guys," I called to the group. "My guide would like to sing a song for you."

We gathered all the people around. Mohammed stood up on a little box he had found, then he looked at me and said, "Start me off, Lori. Like one, two. One, two, three."

I started him off, and Mohammed sang at the top of his lungs—off-key, of course:

> God is so good.
> God is so good.
> God is so good,
> He's so good to me.

Our whole group cheered and clapped, and Mohammed stood there with a huge smile on his face. He looked at me and said, "Lori, I am good singer!"

After everybody left, I said, "Yes, Mohammed, you are a good singer. But did you know that God loves you? He died on the cross and wants to give you life."

"Lori, I do not know about that," Mohammed said, "but I do know this ..." and he opened his mouth to sing again.

"No! OK, OK, Mohammed, I know what you know!"

He got on his horse and rode off. As I watched him go, I said to the Lord, "Please, God, will You use that song in his life someday when he's questioning the purpose and the meaning of his existence? Bring back to his mind the fact that You're so good, so good to him."

We must each find the ministry God has for us, then be willing to overcome every barrier thrown before us to be faithful to that ministry. A life lived for oneself can never be a truly balanced life.

> *You have a ministry. However insignificant it may seem to you, it is very significant to God.*

To have a spiritually balanced life, we must combine our times of solitude and silent worship with times of joyful Christian fellowship and group worship. We should balance emphasis on ourselves and our own Christian walk with service to others. We need to develop our strengths, gifts, and special abilities. We hear a great deal about how important it is to develop our weak points, and certainly that is a good thing to do, but I strongly believe in spending the majority of our time developing to the max those areas of ourselves that are already strong. Others' strengths lie in the very areas that are weak for us, and those people can perform there much better than we will ever be able to perform. So, our best course lies in letting others minister in those areas where we are weakest, while we, in turn, concentrate on those abilities with which God has gifted us.

Spiritual Mentoring

Every young believer needs someone who has walked this way before and is willing to reach out and lend a hand to guide him or her along. Baby Christians need mature Christians who can help them toward a better knowledge of God. Such a helper is a spiritual mentor. If you do not need one, you need to be one.

> The church is meant to be a community of spiritual friends and spiritual directors who journey together to God. We must become that community. Prayer is the starting point.
>
> —Larry Crabb
> *The Safest Place on Earth*

An Attitude of Servanthood

An attitude of servanthood enables us, by the power of the Holy Spirit, to submit to the Lord and serve Him by serving others with humility and joy. When we have the right kind of servant attitude, we will not be easily offended by cynical, critical people, or upset when the ones we serve don't appreciate us. When it comes right down to it, the Lord is the only one we serve. So, what difference do the praises and affirmations of people make? That's not to say we don't appreciate and enjoy the support and encouragement of others. Of course we do. Yet in true servanthood we can live and serve without it. The Lord's affirmation is enough.

Certainly one aspect of servanthood is developing a meaningful volunteer life, giving out with nothing tangible coming back in return. This might be done under the auspices of a Christian organization, but it doesn't have to be. To do something that takes time and effort on our part and expect nothing in return adds a sense of purpose and meaning to our lives.

When I was seventeen, I got my driver's license. All I could think of was driving—anywhere, anytime. So I said to my mom, "I'd like to use our car."

"Well, Lori," Mom said, "you're new with your license. You can't just go out and drive the city. You have to have a reason."

"Well, uh, I do have a reason," I said.

"Oh? And what is it?"

"Umm, well," I stammered, "I'm going to go visit ... the nursing home."

My mom said, "OK. That warrants the car."

So I got out the phone book and looked up "Nursing Home." I jotted down an address, got in the VW, and went to a nearby nursing home in Vancouver, Washington. I walked in, went to the desk, and said to the nurses there, "My name is Lori Marvel" (that's what it was at the time), "and I'm seventeen years old. I wanted to get out and use the car, so I told my parents I was going to come and visit your nursing home. I have just an hour, and I was wondering if you could give me the name of someone who never has anyone to visit him or her."

The nurses looked at each other. Then one said, "Well, welcome to our home. You can visit anyone here. They don't have visitors—maybe a couple—but most of them have none. We're not the high-class nursing home that most people put their parents in."

"So I can just go into a room and visit?" I asked.

"That's right," the nurse said.

I went into the first room I saw, and there was a lady lying in bed. "Hi!" I said. "I just wanted to come in and meet you and talk for a while. Can you tell me about your day?"

She stared at me. "Ummmm," she said. Then, "Do you want money?"

"No," I said, "I don't want money. I just want to make a new friend. My name is Lori and I wanted to use the car, so I decided to come and talk to you. What is your name?"

"Mrs. Smith," she said. Then, "Honey, how much do you charge to visit me?"

"No, no, Mrs. Smith," I said. "I don't want any money."

"Are you taking a survey?"

"No!" I said. "I'm seventeen years old, and ... you know what? I really need a new friend. So I'm wondering if you'd be my friend."

"You're sure you don't want any money?"

"Positive."

"Well, then, I'll tell you about me," Mrs. Smith said. "I used to be a schoolteacher. Back then we'd have all the kids in one room, and I'd teach ..." She started telling me her story. It was wonderful.

Finally I interrupted her to say, "I have to go now, Mrs. Smith, but I just wanted to tell you—I really am enjoying having you for my new friend."

"Little one," she said, "when you leave, would you do me a favor?"

"Sure," I said.

"Would you get one foot outside of my door and one foot inside my room, and as loud as you can, say, 'Good-bye, Mrs. Smith! I love you! I'll come back and see you again!'

You don't really have to come back and see me, Sweetheart. But won't you just say it anyway for me?"

"Why do you want me to do that?" I asked.

"Oh, Sweetheart, because you're my first visitor in so long. And I haven't heard anybody tell me that they love me and would want to come back to see me. And I'd just ... I'd like to hear it. And I want everyone else to hear it, too."

So I got halfway out in the hallway, halfway in the room, and I said in a loud voice, "Good-bye, Mrs. Smith! I love you! I'll come back and see you again!"

"Louder, child, louder!" Mrs. Smith said.

"GOOD-BYE, MRS. SMITH! I LOVE YOU! I'LL COME BACK AND SEE YOU AGAIN!"

I wept all the way home. Through the rest of my high school years, every Tuesday and Thursday I was in that nursing home, going from room to room. And God began to teach me that in life I had to give out, not wanting anything in return.

You might want to go to a nursing home, or you may prefer to volunteer somewhere else. Here are some ideas to consider:

- Volunteer to take care of someone's kids and give their parents a night off.
- Volunteer to help out at the local boys' or girls' club.
- Get some friends together and clean up a roadway (or a park or a beach).
- Help out in a school classroom. There are many ways to make yourself useful there, from making photocopies to

grading papers to helping a child with his or her homework to sharing your own personal expertise with a classroom.

- If you're good at home repairs, offer to help older people and those who can't afford to hire the work done.
- Go ahead and visit a nursing home once in a while. You never know, you might be there yourself one day.

You may think of something completely different. Fine. But whatever you decide to do, do it faithfully and develop a meaningful volunteer life. Giving when you get nothing tangible in return will add a special dimension of balance to your life.

I never look at the masses as my responsibility. I look at the individual. I can love only one person at a time. I can feed only one person at a time. Just one, one, one. You get closer to Christ by coming closer to each other. As Jesus said, "Whatever you do to the least of my brethren, you do to me." So you begin ... I begin. I picked up one person. Maybe if I didn't pick up that one person I wouldn't have picked up 42,000. The whole work is only a drop in the ocean. But if I didn't put the drop in, the ocean would be one drop less.

—Mother Teresa
Words to Love By

Once you are working toward balance in your spiritual life, you will be ready to move on to balancing your physical life.

Balance Journal

Entitle this section of your journal *Spiritual Balance*, then—

- Write down your thoughts on each of the following questions:
  How do I react to the daily ups and downs in my life?
  How could I react in a healthier way?
  How might I be more serene?
  How might I demonstrate a more balanced approach?

- Put a check beside the things in the following list that you might add to your life, and make notations on how and when you might accomplish each one.

  ☐ Set aside quiet time for prayer every day.
  ☐ Join a Bible study.
  ☐ Make a list of uplifting and thought-provoking books I want to read.
  ☐ Make a list of books that can help me achieve more spiritual balance.
  ☐ Begin to plan toward going away on a spiritual retreat.
  ☐ Share my spiritual life with others.

☐ Identify times in my life when God has faithfully provided for me.

☐ Find a spiritual mentor.

☐ Be a spiritual mentor.

- Read David's prayer in Psalm 27:4-8.

- David's one request was to be in the presence of God. Pray for a heart attuned to consistent communion with God.

Chapter 3

Physical Balance

People are always telling me how they think I should act. I have heard it all:

- "Lori, don't be so dramatic."
- "Don't talk to strangers, Lori."
- "Lori, you need to cross-stitch, knit, and have babies instead of climbing mountains, riding bikes, and going parachuting."
- "Lori, you talk too much. Try and be more like a lady."

As a young woman, I was even sent to two different charm schools. Neither one took. When I tried being all the things people told me I should be, I felt as if I were in a strait-jacket. Then one day I realized something important: *God did not create me to be all those things.* So I burst out of all the constraints, and I have never regretted it for a minute.

That's not to say I don't see room for improvement. I certainly do. Yet I want to make those improvements in keeping with who God created me to be. God has His own perspective of me, and that's the only perspective that matters.

Not everybody likes me, but that's OK. There's only one Lori Salierno in this universe (*Thank goodness for that!* you may be thinking), and I am going to be the best Lori Salierno I can be.

Being the best I can be starts with remembering that my body is a temple of God. I don't dare let it get run-down, shabby, lumpy, or weak. That's the reason this chapter is so important to me.

Let's talk about the things that will keep God's temples— our bodies—appropriate places for Him to reside: eating well, exercising, getting a sufficient amount of rest, and dressing appropriately.

Eat Right

Let me guess: Being the busy person you are, more nights than you intend, you end up at a fast-food place, ordering hamburgers. You're overweight, but, hey, who isn't? Exercise? Please! It's all you can do to drag yourself home at night, and you sure don't want to waste your weekend groaning and puffing over some boring exercise machine. You're tired at night, but between finishing up office work and doing the endless jobs that need to be done at home, you are lucky to be able to plop down in front of the television before nine or ten o'clock. And it takes a bit of watching for you to unwind enough to sleep.

Am I at least partly right? I thought so!

Well, let's talk about your upkeep of the temple God has

entrusted to you, and let's start with what you put into it to keep it going. That's right—food.

Most of us know that a nutritious, well-balanced diet is important, especially when we're under stress. We also know that eating too much of the wrong thing—or even of the right thing—will cause us to gain weight, and that too much weight is unhealthy. In fact, the majority of us have at one time or another been on a weight-loss diet. We all have seen the pictures of the stick-thin models in magazines and catalogues that are supposed to represent the ideal body shape. So what is the answer? Diet!

Actually, as many of us know by experience, diets seldom work. What dieting does do is lower the rate at which your body burns calories. Even if you cut to bare minimum and feed your body a mere five hundred calories a day, it doesn't work. That's because your body automatically goes into starvation mode. It thinks it's dying, and since it desperately wants to survive, it slows down and burns calories at a much slower rate than normal. It seems strange, but if we want to burn fat we have to take in enough quality calories to give our bodies the energy to do fat-burning work.

Instead of thinking *diet*, think *lifestyle*. The way to get your body at its peak is to embrace balance in your life. Change the way you eat. Learn what is healthful, and then apply what you have learned. Not only will your body change in positive ways now, but your new habits will make those changes a part of you for the rest of your life.

> *The only diet that really works is the one you can stick to for the rest of your life.*

When it comes to weight, be realistic. To look like a fashion model is unrealistic (not to mention downright dangerous) for the vast majority of us. To want to look thirty-five when you are fifty-five is unrealistic. To hope to be tall and slender when your parents and grandparents are short and plump is unrealistic. To decide to lose thirty pounds before your high school reunion two months from now is unrealistic.

If you pursue an unrealistic goal, you will undoubtedly become discouraged and give up on the whole thing. It is helpful to choose a range to work within rather than a set amount. ("I want to be able to wear a smaller clothing size by the high school reunion.")

Once you reach your maximum weight, take action to prevent yourself from going any higher. Refuse to accept excuses from yourself about weight gain. If you are brutal with five pounds now, you will never have to deal with twenty pounds later.

Healthy Nuggets

Most of us know the basic habits for healthful eating. We have seen food pyramids. We know that fast foods and sweet treats are not good for us. We have heard all about the evils of deep-fat fried foods. Yet when we are hungry and those things are calling out our names, it's awfully hard to resist. Here are some tips that will help make the battle easier:

- Keep plenty of nutritious ready-to-eat foods in your pantry and refrigerator.
- Stay away from refined sugar and high-carbohydrate foods; they lead to the storage of excess fat in your body.
- Don't buy that tempting junk food "just to have it on hand for others." If you shouldn't eat it, don't buy it. (The "others" shouldn't eat it either, by the way.)
- Drink lots of water, at least eight eight-ounce glasses per day.
- Bake, broil, or roast instead of frying. (Also keep this guideline in mind when you order out.)
- Never shop for groceries when you're hungry. Your willpower will be at its lowest.
- Eat when you're hungry and stop when you're full. (Yes, even if there is food left on your plate.)
- Take small bites.
- Eat slowly.
- When you're dying for a snack, wait ten minutes before giving in. The desire just might pass.
- Pack your own snacks when you're traveling.
- If you eat a large, rich meal one day, be especially careful the next day.

Make Time for Exercise

In a healthy, balanced lifestyle, exercise is indispensable. When we exercise, our bodies produce endorphins, a natural substance that can give a feeling of well-being. Exercise also serves as an outlet for stress, and it sets in motion biochemical changes that speed up our bodies' ability to burn calories. Exercise builds muscles, and muscle burns more calories than fat. That means that even when we aren't actually exercising, we are still burning calories faster than before we started exercising.

So if exercise is so great, how come we don't all do it?

- Because it's too hot.
- Because we're too tired.
- Because the kids have the sniffles, or they're cranky, or they get bored.
- Because the gym's too crowded or it's too far away.
- Because we're going to, but not today.
- Because of any one of a thousand other reasons.

Listen to these procrastinators. Do any of them sound like you?

JACK: *"I'm going to start exercising when my friend Dave does. I'm working on a project at the office right now that keeps me there late nearly every evening, but once that's done I'll try to get Dave going with me."*

It's wonderful to get encouragement from your friends and family, and it's certainly true that difficult circumstances can hinder your schedule. Yet the bottom line is that it is up to you to set aside the time to start a lifetime of fitness. If your excuse is anything like Jack's, I suggest that you write down your exercise schedule on your calendar right alongside your other important appointments. Come up with a realistic schedule, then stick to it, no matter what. Never cancel your exercise session. If you can't possibly make it at the scheduled time, reschedule it for later that day, or the next day at the latest.

RUTHANNE: *"I am going to get started, but I feel like I may be coming down with a cough."*

Unless you really are certifiably sick, this is called procrastination. When it comes time to exercise, it is the most common ailment known. Don't wait until you feel great and you have the energy. (That's more likely to be *after* you exercise.) Just get ready and do it!

CHRISTINE: *"I tried exercising. I went to the gym every other day for three weeks, and I didn't lose a pound! It just doesn't seem to work for me."*

Some people expect to see immediate weight loss and an increase in their strength and body tone after only one session. When they realize that working out requires slow, steady commitment in order to achieve any real gain, they become discouraged. Focus on rewards other than immediate weight loss, such as a lowering of your stress and an improvement in your energy level.

NICK: *"I don't get it. Every time I get started on an exercise routine, I injure myself and can't continue."*

No wonder. Nick dives headlong into a challenging new regimen and ends up overdoing it. Then, in pain, he cannot go back for so long that he gives up. If this sounds familiar, try setting more realistic goals for yourself, then pare them down a step further. So what if you leave the gym knowing you could have done more? Then you'll be anxious to come back tomorrow and *do* more.

Many people feel guilty or stressed because they know they "should" exercise regularly, but they just don't want to. Exercise can be strenuous and monotonous, to be sure, and when you're over your head in daily responsibilities, it's even more difficult to tie on those athletic shoes and head for a workout. The secret is to develop a realistic strategy for fitting exercise into your specific lifestyle.

The benefits of regular exercise far outweigh the time, trouble, and sweat you will have to invest. Instead of thinking of the time you are spending, think about ...

- boosting your energy
- relieving stress
- keeping your appetite in check

- building a higher metabolism
- creating strong muscles and bones
- strengthening your heart
- achieving better weight control
- improving your sleep

When you take all of this into consideration, regular exercise is pretty much worth it, don't you think?

Exercise Personality

One person loves running, another detests it. One loves beach volleyball at lunchtime, another couldn't care less. Just as in every other area of our lives, when it comes to exercise, each of us is different. We each have our own exercise personality. Below are listed some of the exercise problems that beleaguer us, followed by some suggestions for getting around those barriers:

Problem: Monotonous exercises drive you crazy with boredom.
Solution: Choose an exercise you can combine with something that will keep you intellectually stimulated, such as riding a stationary bike or a stair climber. This will allow you to read or watch television while you work out.

Problem: Exercise for the sake of exercise isn't fulfilling.
Solution: Try something that can allow you to express your creativity, such as figure skating or swing dancing.

Problem: You need a challenge to make the exercise interesting.
Solution: Go for fast-paced, think-on-your-feet activities, like racquetball, tennis, or downhill skiing.

Problem: You get encouragement and energy from exercising with others.
Solution: You might join a class (such as aerobics) or get involved in a team sport (softball or volleyball, for instance). Besides being fun, being accountable to others will keep you going.

Problem: You enjoy competition.
Solution: Play team sports, such as soccer or tennis.

Problem: You do *not* enjoy competition.
Solution: Stick with solo sports, such as biking, running, and swimming.

Even when you find something you enjoy, there will likely be times when you feel too busy, rushed, or tired to exercise. When that happens, use these "tricks" to help pump up your motivation:

1. *See exercise as NONoptional.* The minute you allow yourself to argue about going, you increase your chances of settling into a sedentary lifestyle. Would you skip work because you couldn't think of what to wear? Would you stop brushing your teeth because you're too tired at night? People make time for their nonoptionals. Make exercise one of yours.

2. *Reward yourself.* Get a new music tape to listen to while you exercise. Pick up a new magazine or a good book to read while you ride the exercise cycle. Treat yourself to a smoothie fruit drink (with added protein) after you finish a vigorous exercise.

3. *Trick yourself.* Tell yourself, "Today I'll work out for only fifteen minutes." You'll find that once you get going, practically every time you'll keep on until you've put in much more than your minimum time.

4. *Use your spare moments.* On the days you don't exercise, use the oft-repeated tried and true techniques for getting unplanned exercise. Park in a far corner of the parking lot so you will have to walk to and from your car. Never use an elevator if there are stairs. Do stretches and calisthenics before you go to bed.

5. *Set realistic short-term goals.* Forget that twenty-five pounds you need to lose. Set a goal to swim an extra lap, ride the exercise bike an extra five minutes (or raise the intensity a notch), or walk all the way to the top of the hill in your neighborhood instead of just to the corner. Do sit-ups while you watch the evening news. Then take pride in achieving those smaller goals.

6. *Use your lunch break.* Instead of eating in the lunchroom—or even worse, working through lunch—use part of the time to take a brisk walk or maybe even ride a bicycle.

"But," you may be saying, "I hardly have any time with my family the way it is. If I start on a regular exercise program, I'll never see them."

Good point. If you have this problem, why not exercise together with them? Look at the suggestions below and put a check beside the ones that might work for your family.

☐ Walk or jog while you push a stroller.

☐ Ride along with your kids when they ride their bikes.

☐ Use an exercise bike in front of the television when you are watching a family video.

☐ Try a family sport, such as hiking or skiing.

☐ Plan family outings in places where you can walk or hike.

☐ Take family neighborhood walks.

☐ Play sports as a family (softball, basketball, bowling).

Do you not know that your body is a temple of the Holy Spirit, who is in you, whom you have received from God?

1 CORINTHIANS 6:19

When we think of exercising, we think of going to a gym or playing a sport or jogging early in the morning. Yet the opportunity to exercise comes our way all the time. Supplement your official exercise routine with easy exercises throughout the day. Try:

1. making it a policy to ignore those close parking places.

2. doing your own yard work.

3. playing active games with your kids, such as basketball, jump-rope, tag, or hopscotch.

4. taking a walk with a friend instead of talking over a cup of coffee and a piece of pie.

5. riding your bike to the store.

6. walking up a few flights of stairs to an appointment instead of getting on the elevator.

7. doing sit-ups and stretching exercises while you watch television.

8. doing isometric exercises (tighten your stomach, buttocks, and thighs) while you drive.

9. mixing cake batter by hand instead of using an electric mixer.

10. washing your own car.

11. making the most of those irritating delays (going for a brisk walk at the airport, walking around the block while you wait for your lunch partner to show up, or walking up and down an extra flight of stairs if you arrive early for an appointment).

12. carrying your own luggage.

13. walking to lunch instead of driving.

14. doing fifty crunches before you go to bed.

15. walking whenever and wherever you can.

Even if you agree with everything I've said, even if you've made a commitment to yourself, and even if you desperately want your body to be the best temple it can be, you will likely have some difficulty sticking to your exercise regimen. Almost all of us do.

It will help if you become aware of your own excuses for skipping exercise. For instance, if at the end of a busy day you are just too tired, try exercising at lunchtime or early in the morning. It may also help to make appointments to exercise with friends. If you are accountable to someone else, it is a lot more difficult to back out at the last minute. If you miss a day, forgive yourself and get right back into your routine. It *will* pay off. So give yourself credit up front, even before you see the pounds coming off.

Exercise is one of the most worthwhile investments of time and energy that you can make, and it doesn't have to cost you a bundle. You don't need a great exercise wardrobe, state-of-the-art equipment, or a membership in an exclusive gym. All you need is a willingness to find what works best for you and a determination to keep at it. You won't be sorry!

Get Enough Rest

The frenzied activity of our busy schedules, day in and day out, leaves most of us physically drained. "Work hard and you will succeed," we are told by our society. So we allow work to dominate our lives and squeeze out other crucial needs, including rest. We even tend to play hard, so that when we finish our recreation, we are more tired than ever.

We need true physical rest, and that includes enough time not only for relaxing leisure but also for sleep. If we are to properly care for the temple that God has entrusted to each of us, we must ensure our physical rest by refusing to overwork and overschedule.

How often have you been reciting a litany of your busy, involved life and been interrupted by someone asking, "Do you ever have time to sleep?" What was your answer? Did you laugh? Did you brag about being able to get along on five hours of sleep?

Unfortunately, many of us don't put much value on sleep. That's too bad. Research shows that far too many of us aren't getting enough. We need between eight and ten hours a night—an hour or two more than most of us are getting. Some say that statistic is changing for the better, which would be a real boon to many of us. Less fatigue can increase our ability to deal with stress, and will also increase our resistance to disease.

Sleep, that once rare commodity in stressed-out America, is the new status symbol. Once derided as a wimpish failing ... slumber is now being touted as the restorative companion to the creative mind.

—Nancy Jeffrey
Wall Street Journal

Sabbath Rest

Sleep isn't the only kind of rest we need. We also need to *vacate* (vacation) and to *recreate* (recreation). As Christians we learn about the necessity of taking one day a week to rest from the usual stresses and concerns of life, and we often think of this break as a spiritual concern. It is, of course, but did you know that it also makes good physical sense? Getting away—really away—from our hectic schedules allows us to vacate and recreate, to literally restore our bodies.

So, what types of guidelines should you use for your day of Sabbath rest? First of all, make it a rule that you will do no occupational work on that day. Beyond that, make a list of those things that will give you a sense of joyful rest. Consider such things as:

- Taking a nap
- Enjoying a leisurely walk
- Having a special (low-work) meal with your family or close friends
- Relaxing and doing nothing
- Lying on the couch and listening to music
- Reading a book
- Playing a game
- Sitting and talking over a cup of coffee
- Reading the Bible
- Doing spiritual study

If something you try is not restful to you, cross it off your list. When something else occurs to you, add it and give it a try.

When you go to bed rested and revived, do your best to take the feeling of Sabbath rest into the week ahead.

Make the Most of What You Have

Some of us are short and some are tall. Some are skinny and others are plump. Some have big feet, straight hair (or no hair!), a big nose, or some other feature we dislike. Yet whatever our physical attributes—or drawbacks—we can make the most of what we have.

A sweet Christian man by the name of Martin was badly burned in a terrible fire. His face is scarred, his ears and nose are mangled, and his fingers are gone. Yet few who know him would call him anything but attractive. To a large degree, this is because of his wonderful spirit and attitude. Yet he has also learned the secret of making the most of the temple with which God has entrusted him.

As an ambassador of God, you can and should do the same. What do I mean? Well, here are some thoughts for starters:

- **Stay up-to-date in your dress and appearance.** Too often Christians have a reputation of being behind the times and frumpy.
- **If you don't have a knack for putting clothes and outfits together, go shopping with someone who does.** Of course,

you will want this to be someone whose taste you like and whose idea of necessities are not items that will completely blow your clothing budget for months to come.

- **Whatever your clothing budget, spend the money wisely.** Many people get talked into buying something expensive that really is not that important to them. Another big trap is sales. Yes, sales. That's because it's easy to see something that is too good a price to pass up, even though it may not look good on us or we may have absolutely nothing to wear with it.

- **Expand your wardrobe by trading with a friend.** That outfit you are sick of will be new and exciting to someone else, and there may well be something stuck in the back of her closet that will go just perfectly with something you have.

- **Wear colors that make you feel good.** It's amazing how much a color that pleases you will improve your confidence and sense of well-being, and believe me, that will show.

- **Make sure the clothes you buy are returnable.** You know how it is. In the store it seems fine—maybe even better than fine. Yet when you get home it just doesn't look right. Don't finalize the purchase until you are able to see how the item looks and feels in the comfort of your own bedroom, in front of your own mirror.

Yes, there certainly are far more important things than how you look. But the fact is, when you look your best you will feel your best, and when you feel your best you are more likely to do your best.

Give Credit Where Credit Is Due

All of us, from the most attractive to the most ... well ... not attractive, need to practice changing our attitude toward our physical appearance. Here are some things to keep firmly in mind:

- Every day do one particular thing in terms of nutrition, exercise, and appearance to help you become your physical best. Don't let these things fall to the bottom of your to-do list. Becoming your physical best is a lifelong, daily process.
- Your physical best means *your* physical best, not someone else's. Accept who you are and give thanks for it.
- Look in your daily routine for hidden opportunities to exercise.
- Make it a goal to break your bad habits.
- Practice looking your best even if you are just with your family. For whom is it more important to look your best?
- See yourself as a work in progress, and take pleasure in the changes you see.

> You can't break a bad habit by throwing it out the window. You've got to walk it slowly down the stairs.
>
> —Mark Twain

Goals and pointers that move you toward improvement are wonderful, but don't get so buried in them that you neglect to look at what you have accomplished and to celebrate it. Give credit where credit is due. Whenever you pass a mirror, notice something attractive about yourself. Accept that you are you and no one else, and quit making comparisons. In fact, make a commitment to avoid commenting on other people's physical appearances. Stay away from magazines that make you feel depressed with yourself, and focus instead on seeing yourself as God sees you.

> The Lord does not look at the things man looks at. Man looks at the outward appearance, but the Lord looks at the heart.
>
> 1 Samuel 16:7

Be in Touch With Yourself

A very good rule for achieving physical balance is this: Listen to your body. When you feel tired, rest. When you are hungry, eat—but wisely—and when you are full, stop eating. If there is something that constantly pulls you down, take a vacation from it.

When you are tempted to doubt the value of the temple God has entrusted to you, reaffirm yourself by reading (or reciting) these words from Psalm 139:13-16:

For You created my inmost being;
   you knit me together in my mother's womb.
I praise you because I am fearfully and wonderfully
   made;
   your works are wonderful,
   I know that full well.
My frame was not hidden from you when I was made
   in the secret place.
When I was woven together in the depths of the earth,
   your eyes saw my unformed body.
All the days ordained for me were written in Your
   book before one of them came to be.

Balance Journal

Make a new heading called *Physical Balance*. Then,

* Write out your thoughts on each of the following questions:
   How long has it been since I had a physical exam?
   How much exercise do I get each day? Each week?
   What types of exercise do I enjoy?
   What foods energize me?
   What foods cause me problems?
   How much sleep do I get at night?
   How might I demonstrate a more balanced approach
   to my physical life?

- Read the following quotation from George McDonald:

  I would rather be what God chose to make me than the most glorious creature that I could think of; for to have been thought about, born in God's thought, and then made by God, is the dearest, grandest, and most precious thing in all thinking.

- Write down your thoughts about this statement.

Chapter 4

Mental Balance

One of the most difficult types of balance for many of us to achieve is mental balance. When we were little, everything was new and there was much to keep our brains active. As we grew older, we were in school. We read, we were constantly exposed to new people, new things, and new ideas. Yet when we reach adulthood and get busy with jobs, families, and all of our many involvements, it is tempting to put our brains on a shelf and take it easy.

What a shame!

Every one of us is constantly changing, and the world around us is constantly changing, too. Aren't those reasons enough to become lifelong learners?

If you still aren't convinced, think about this: Whatever dominates our thoughts long enough will become the dominant passion in our lives.

Wow! We dare not let our minds drift into neutral.

Why should you constantly expose yourself to new things? Because learning leads to learning. Once you get started, you will discover interests you never knew you had. Suddenly you will have something to occupy your mind when you would otherwise be bored and irritated. (Instead of standing impatiently in line at the grocery store, for instance, you may find yourself engrossed in reading the labels on your purchases, now that you are more aware of your nutritional needs.) Imagine the sense of accomplishment you will get from the new areas of information opened up to you.

Sally and Andrew are a good example. Two years ago, already in their late sixties, they were sure their years of learning were behind them. Then their grandchildren began talking to them about computers, e-mail, and the Internet. "It was like the children were speaking a foreign language," Sally confesses. "We just told them, Grandma and Grandpa are too old to learn to use a computer."

Then Jesse, their oldest grandchild, went off to college on the other side of the country. "We missed him terribly," Andrew recalls. "He was too busy to write and too poor to telephone. We called him, but he was always out."

When Jesse came home for Christmas, he told his grandparents, "If you just had e-mail we could really keep in touch. I could let you know about all my classes, tell you what happened during the day, tell you about my friends ... everything."

Sally and Andrew began to wonder if it just might be possible for them to learn to use the computer, or at least the e-mail function, which the kids told them anyone could do. Some friends gave them a used computer, and their grandchildren went to work giving them lessons.

"That was five years and two computers ago," Andrew says. "Today we are almost experts. We surf the Web, we communicate with missionaries around the world, we have traced our family trees ... oh, yes, and we 'talk' with each of our grandkids at least once a week. And Jesse is now in Germany!"

Yet there is another benefit to this experience that Sally and Andrew probably don't even realize. They are modeling for their grandchildren the value of learning at any age.

Learn to use a computer. Teach yourself a new language. Learn to play a new game. Discover a new author. It doesn't matter *what* you learn as much as the fact that you are learning.

I expect I shall be a student to the end of my days.
—Anton Chekhov

Memorizing God's Word

Having said that the fact of learning is more important than the actual subject matter learned, let me suggest that one of the best ways to bring mental balance into your life is to memorize Scripture. Not only will you get the advantage of keeping your brain active and stimulated, you will also have the joy of filling your mind with the revealed Word of God.

You will find that memorized Scripture will bring a surprising strength to your mind and a wonderful perspective to your life. It is one of the best ways to help you determine what your priorities are. And here's a bonus: no matter what your lifestyle, Scripture memorization can be fit into it. Write the portions you choose to commit to memory on 3x5 cards, and use those cards to help you. If you commute to work, use your time at red lights to read over the cards. If you work at home, keep the cards beside you, at your desk, by the telephone, or wherever. Keep copies in the bathroom—you can review them while you shave or while you blow-dry your hair. In the kitchen you can review them while you mash the potatoes and stir the soup, and then again while you wash the dishes.

The four "R's" of memorizing Scripture are:

- Read
- Repeat
- Recite
- Review

Let's look at each of these separately:

Read the Scripture out loud. What does the passage mean? Why was it written? Read it again, adding an annotation to it that will help you understand the tone in which it was written. Now read it over several times.

Repeat that Scripture again and again, one phrase at a time. This is where the passage really gets embedded into your mind. Repeat it over and over until you can say it by memory.

Recite the Scripture by memory. Don't worry if you stumble. Just refresh your memory, then start again. Practice saying the whole passage out loud from memory until you can do it easily.

Review the Scripture daily. This will make certain that it is permanently etched in your mind. You will be surprised at the unexpected times when Scripture passages will come back to you.

Some of you are saying, "That sounds great, but memorizing Scripture is too hard for me. I can't memorize. I'm just not good at that kind of thing."

Don't be so sure. There is no such thing as a bad memory, only an underdeveloped memory. Your memory is like a muscle. The more you use it, the stronger and more capable it becomes. So the thing to do is to start using it. Begin to develop your "memory power" and just see how much you can do.

It may be more accurate to say that you don't memorize Scripture simply because there are other things that take higher priority in your life. Again, it's up to you to determine what is really important. Sure, you will be tempted to give up. You will be tempted to spend that commute time listening to the car radio and your dishwashing time listening to the evening news on television. But again, it is a matter of priorities. You can choose to get rid of those temptations (turn off the car radio) or to deal with them (close the kitchen door so you are not pulled into the evening news that your spouse is watching in the family room).

One goal of the *read, repeat, recite, review* method of Scripture memorization is to strive for word-perfect memorization. Something that has been extremely helpful to me has been finding a friend to whom I can be accountable, both in my Scripture memorization and in my Christian walk. By learning and reciting together, each of us not only has someone who is counting on us, but we have someone with whom we can discuss the Scripture. We have been able to share fresh insights and beautiful illustrations, as well as specific ways in which the Scripture has spoken to us.

Here are some other suggestions to help you in your Scripture memorization:

- Work on it during a time when your mind is not churning with other things (not when your boss is making demands, for instance, or when your children are clamoring for dinner). Many people find that attacking it first thing in the morning works especially well.

- Memorize the Scripture reference with the passage. If you don't do this, there will be times when you will find yourself struggling to locate just where in the Bible a particular verse can be found.

- Write the verse out. Writing helps to get it fixed in your mind. Again, it is nice to have several copies on 3x5 cards that you can post in places where you will see them regularly. Each time you catch a glimpse of a verse card, read the passage.

- Say the verses out loud. Speaking the verses audibly does a lot more to encourage memorization than repeating them silently in your mind.
- Continue to review earlier verses even as you learn new ones. You don't want to give yourself a chance to forget them.

So where should you begin your memorization? I suggest that you start with Philippians 4:8. In the New International Version (NIV) it reads this way:

Finally, brothers, whatever is true,
whatever is noble,
whatever is right,
whatever is pure,
whatever is lovely,
whatever is admirable—
if anything is excellent or praiseworthy—
think about such things.

I'm sure you can immediately tell why I think it is an excellent one to store in your mind.

Although there are many wonderful verses to commit to memory, please don't limit yourself to learning only isolated verses. Be open to tackling whole sections. They may look a bit intimidating at first glance, but you will find that they will give you a better sense of the flow and impact of the Scripture. Here are some specific sections that I would like to suggest you try:

- Psalm 23
- Romans 8:35-39
- Micah 6:6-12

I guarantee that once you get started, you won't want to stop.

I know of no other single practice in the Christian life more rewarding, practically speaking, than memorizing Scripture. That's right. No other single discipline is more useful and rewarding than this. No other single exercise pays greater spiritual dividends! Your prayer life will be strengthened. Your attitudes and outlook will begin to change. Your mind will become alert and observant. Your confidence and assurance will be enhanced. Your faith will be solidified.

—Charles R. Swindoll
Growing Strong in the Seasons of Life

Learning for a Lifetime

There are so many things I want to learn. There are so many books I want to read, so many people I want to know about, so many places I want to become acquainted with, so many ideas I want to hear about. How about you? Do you want to keep on learning for the rest of your life? I am almost certain you are nodding your head "yes." Very few people actually *want* to stagnate in life. Yet, unfortunately, many people end up doing just that. Why?

There are ten major barriers to ongoing learning. Let's look at each of them.

1. **Procrastination.** Yep, it's that same old problem rearing its ugly head again. We are constantly besieged by the temptation to put it off until we have more time. That will never happen, and if you wait for it, you will stagnate with the words "someday" on your lips.

2. **No follow-through.** You say you have good intentions? Great. But please understand, they are worth nothing if you don't act on them.

3. **Lack of preparation**. "Oh, no. I was going to take that class. I didn't realize it was today!" Many people miss out on opportunities to learn because they don't prepare. If there is a deadline, meet it. If there is a date, write it on your calendar. Make learning one of your priorities.

4. **Complacency.** Many people are convinced that they already know enough. They do OK the way they are, so why push themselves? That's an unfortunate attitude, because there is so much more available, and you never know what is coming tomorrow. Sally and Andrew were doing all right, too, but if they hadn't

learned to use the computer, they would have missed out on so much with their grandchildren.

5. **Unrealistic expectations**. "I tried it, but I can't learn." Really? If this is your excuse, the problem may well be that you made the mistake of assuming you could pick up a new skill immediately. None of us can. We do not learn as easily as we once did, and we don't learn as quickly as our children do. Yet that doesn't mean we can't learn. It just means we need to cut ourselves some slack. Each of us learns and progresses at a different rate.

6. **Quitting too soon**. Discouragement always seems to be lurking around the corner. We get frustrated when we see someone else learning faster than we are. Someone makes some crack about our work. We think we are doing well and then we seem to hit a blank wall. Yes, all these things happen. Yet if learning is a high priority, you will pick yourself up and move forward.

7. **Accepting failures.** Failure is a strange thing. It can drive us into the ground with despair or it can be our best teacher. You will have failure; how you handle it is up to you.

8. **Avoiding risks.** One big temptation for many people is to play it safe. That way, they figure, there won't be mistakes to pull them down. Certainly it doesn't make

sense to behave recklessly, but playing it too safe is boring and gives you no chance to grow.

9. **Saving energy.** Another big temptation is to automatically assume your energy will be better spent somewhere else. In other words, stay within the things you "should" be doing and learning and don't waste your resources on frivolous things. Don't allow yourself to get caught in this trap! Discover the adventure and joy of learning something just for the fun of it.

10. **Letting other people discourage you.** "I've always wanted to learn Spanish," a woman I know said. I asked her if she was going to do it and she said, with a sigh, "No. I mentioned it to my family and they all laughed." Don't allow unsupportive people to cause you to give up. What you learn and when is your personal choice. All that really matters is what *you* think is important. Once you make that decision, say "Adios," go off to class, and *do it.*

Whether you think you can or you think you can't, you're right.

—Henry Ford

The Secret of Growing Better

"I want to go back to school, but I'm forty-five years old," a man said. "If it takes me four years, I will be forty-nine by the time I graduate!"

Guess what? In four years that man will be forty-nine whether he goes back to school or not. We all will be older tomorrow than we are today. Next week we will be even older, and next year older still. This is true whether we are twenty-five or forty-five or seventy-five. Life doesn't stand still. Every one of us is constantly growing and changing. It's the changes we make today that will make the difference in whether we are older and wiser tomorrow or just plain older. As long as we live we are going to age. Yet it is how we spend our time now that will determine how we will age.

Are you determined to age well? Good for you! So am I.

A really good place to start is to stretch yourself by taking an educational risk. There are a number of ways you can do this. You might:

- take a class outside the scope of your present interests and expertise
- work toward a degree
- start and lead a book club
- take an art appreciation class
- take an astronomy class
- learn to play an instrument
- learn a new computer program
- take an introductory foreign language class
- take a theology class

Get the idea? With a little thought, you will be able to fill in more ideas of your own. With a little more thought, you will be able to choose an exciting challenge for yourself. Once you get started learning new things, you will find that there is an increase in your skills and confidence, and that will lead you on to still more learning.

A Minute Found

"But I just don't have time!"

No time. This is the most common argument for not accepting a new challenge. It's not a totally unfounded one. Yet all of us—yes, even you—can find some time, if not in hours then at least in minutes. And believe it or not, a minute is enough to sharpen your mind and learn something new.

> We cannot do everything at once, but we can do something at once.
>
> —Calvin Coolidge

Make it a rule to always carry something to read along with you. Keep a supply of crossword puzzles you can take on airplane trips or to appointments when you know you may have to wait. When you are commuting or driving car pools, listen to recorded sermons or books on tape. Bring your weekly magazines or newspapers along to the gym or to the doctor's office. Not only will you sharpen your mind, but you will find that waiting is much less frustrating if you have something to do.

Sharpening your mental powers doesn't have to be work. There are lots of fun brain-trainers. Try some of these:

- Working crossword puzzles.
- Playing Trivial Pursuit or other games that introduce you to new facts.
- Playing checkers, chess, or other strategy games.
- Playing word games such as Scrabble or Scattergories.
- Making up stories for children.
- Engaging in games, such as Taboo, that make you think fast.
- Renting how-to videos that teach you to do something new.
- Renting travel videos, or videos about different countries or cultures.

May I make a suggestion? If you decide you want to be a person who learns for a lifetime, begin to create a *learning atmosphere* around you. Here are some ways to do this:

- Designate a favorite spot for reading, such as a comfortable chair near the window, where the light is good. Keep a good book or a couple of magazines nearby—maybe even under the chair.
- Set up a writing corner with a journal, a couple of pens, and paper for writing notes.

- Keep 3x5 note cards, a pen, and a Bible in a particular place. As verses or passages of Scripture you would like to commit to memory come to mind, jot them down and put them in the same place. Periodically fill out the cards and have them ready for your next Scripture memory session.
- When it comes time for gift giving (birthdays, Christmas, Mother's or Father's Day), ask for books on topics in which you're interested.
- Create a learning idea file. Clip interesting articles, book reviews, or other things on which you might want to follow up. Be sure to review your file periodically.
- Subscribe to at least one weekly newsmagazine and take the time to read it. This will help you keep up with current events, ideas, books, movies, and a variety of other subjects. It will also introduce you to new topics.

The good thing about learning is that you can practice it at any time and in any place. It will fill those small chunks of time you spend waiting in lines, laying over in airports, sitting on planes or in cars, or sitting in the doctor's or dentist's waiting room. It can be fit right into your everyday situations, whatever they may be. You will find classrooms in the strangest of places, and teachers in the most unlikely of people.

Learn from everyone.

—Ben Franklin

Setting Goals

Accidental learning is wonderful and a great use of spare time. Yet the most productive learning of all will occur when you make up your mind to do something, set a goal, then pursue that goal and accomplish it. Again, people are different. I have a way that works for me, but it might not work so well for you. Some people find planning and goal-setting helpful and encouraging. Others would rather live day to day without a lot of thought for the future. Which type of person are you? If you're not sure, check the statements below. Which ones apply to you?

☐ I carefully plan everything I do.
☐ I sometimes plan, but not always.
☐ I make plans for specific activities, like having a party or going on a trip, but I certainly don't chart the course of my life.
☐ I don't plan much of anything unless it's absolutely necessary.

If you checked the first one, you are an avid planner. If you checked the second, you are an organized planner. If you checked the third, you are an under-stress planner. If you checked the last one, you are an organizational avoider.

Each of these has benefits and each has dangers. For instance, what happens when the avid planner has everything worked out perfectly and a storm makes the plans unworkable? On the other hand, what about the man who makes a call the night before the big party to the young woman he expected to take, only to find out she's going with someone who asked her two weeks before?

To get an idea of how this works, make a list of the benefits and dangers you can see to goal-setting:

Benefits   Dangers

_____   _____

_____   _____

_____   _____

_____   _____

_____   _____

_____   _____

From this list, you can get an even better idea of where you fit on the *avid planner* to *organizational avoider* scale.

You can plan more or you can plan less, but you cannot avoid planning completely. Goals are a necessity, not a luxury. Almost all successful people start with a clear definition of their goals.

Many people find it frightening to examine their hopes and dreams too closely. It's easy to say, "I believe in goals, but not now. I'll set them tomorrow when I'm more in the mood and I have more time." If you're not careful, you can put it off and put if off and put it off, and then find yourself wondering why you never accomplish anything.

Even when it comes to goal-setting, however, balance is the name of the game. Many people make the mistake of trying to achieve a dream by sacrificing all the other areas of their life. A man I'll call Matt knows that from personal experience. When he was eight and his sisters were five and two, his father decided to quit his job as a struggling pastor and get a medical degree. He did accomplish that goal, but it took a horrible toll on the family. For eight years, they lived a shoestring existence. Matt's mother cleaned houses and took in laundry in an effort to keep meat on the table. When Matt started high school, he rebelled against everything his parents had stood for. His mother, exhausted and discouraged, left the family. The girls went to live with two different relatives. Matt stayed with his father, but since Dad was never home, Matt was completely unsupervised. He got into all kinds of trouble, finally getting arrested for car theft.

Was Matt's father's goal worth it? Maybe and maybe not. Was the unbalanced way he went after it worth it? When this question was posed to Matt's father, tears filled his eyes. "I lost my family," he said. "What do *you* think?"

Healthy goal-setting goes beyond focusing on just one aspect of your life. It means deciding what you want your entire life to look like. It means seeing your life in balance.

Should you have goals? Absolutely! Not only is it wise but it is a divine assignment. Look at 2 Corinthians 4:16-18: "Therefore we do not lose heart. Though outwardly we are wasting away, yet inwardly we are being renewed day by day. For our light and momentary troubles are achieving for us an eternal glory that far outweighs them all. So we fix our eyes not on what is seen, but on what is unseen. For what is seen is temporary, but what is unseen is eternal."

You *can* keep on learning, because you must. The world is changing faster than ever, and there is so much to keep up with. Even our youngest children are computer savvy. If we don't learn computer basics, we can't even find a book in the library anymore. Card catalogues are a thing of the past; now it is all on computers. And what about our appliances? If the power goes out, nothing works, and when it comes back on, everything needs to be reset. If we cannot program our video recorders, everyone will know when they see them continually blinking 12:00!

If you still are doubting your ability, let me give you one more assignment. Make a list of all the things you have learned in the last month. You'll almost certainly find that your list is much longer than you ever imagined it would be.

Imagination is more important than knowledge.

—Albert Einstein

Balance Journal

There are so many exciting things to learn about. Here are some fun ones to begin with in your journal under the heading of *Mental Balance:*

- Get up and look out the window. Study something out there for one minute and then try to describe it in detail.

- List as many U.S. presidents as you can in one minute.

- Write down the names of all fifty states—or as many as you can in one minute.

- Pick an age between five and twenty-five. Try to remember where you lived at that age, who your friends were, what pets you had, and so forth.

Here are some questions to ask yourself:

- What is the best book I've ever read?

- Why did I like it so much?

- What are five topics I've always wanted to learn more about?

- What are five things I'd like to learn how to do?

- What skills or abilities do I have that I'd like to enhance or improve?

Now think about some long-term possibilities:

- Start a list of books you want to read this year.

- Look into the computer classes offered locally. Which ones look the most interesting?

- Look into available lecture series. Which might you want to sign up for? Is there someone you could ask to join you?

Chapter 5

Emotional Balance

Your neighbors stop by for coffee and a long chat.

Your son badgers you to let him drive the car across town to his friend's house.

Your coworkers want you to join their softball team.

Your brother and sister-in-law want you to join a book discussion group.

Which of these activities will contribute to your emotional balance?

All of them—if you really want to say "yes." None of them—if you really want to say "no." Saying "yes" when you want and need to say "no" is a major energy-drainer, and one of the most common causes of emotional imbalance.

So why do we do it? Why do we say "yes" when we really want to say "no"? Most often it's because of fear, or because of a false sense of obligation. At any rate, it is most unfortunate. Not only is our time wasted, but as we are doing that thing we really don't want to do, resentment builds up in us. That resentment chews away at our energy and self-esteem and destroys our emotional balance.

Often, people lace their requests with flattery ("You are

so good at working with people! I just love the way you can talk to anyone. Oh, if only I had that gift"). Or they use that old standby—guilt ("You're the only one who can do this. Without you, the whole program will be a flop"). It's a good technique. On the first count, it feels good to be indispensable. On the second, it's awful to feel guilty. But the fact is, if you can't do it, they will find someone else. Every day indispensable people get sick, move away, and say "no," and the world hasn't stopped turning yet. No one is really concerned about your priorities except you, and you will feel a greater sense of accomplishment and self-worth by spending your time on those priorities. Remember, it isn't a question of which is good and which is bad. It's a question of which is better than good, and which is best of all.

"That's the problem!" you may be saying. "I can't decide which is the best, and I'm so worried that I'll make the wrong decision."

"If I say no to my neighbors today, maybe I'll never have another chance to get to know them. Maybe they really need to talk."

"My son is young and just got his driver's license, but as he says, he is dependable. Maybe I am being too strict."

"Perhaps the reason I don't enjoy softball is because I never played on a team. It would take time away from my family, but maybe it would be good for me."

"I don't have any interest in the book discussion, but maybe it is a once-in-a-lifetime opportunity to spend some time with my brother and his wife."

Indecision, Worry, and Anxiety

Indecision, worry, and anxiety are negative mental habits that serve no useful purpose. In his Letter to the Philippians (4:6), the apostle Paul wrote: "Do not be anxious about anything, but in everything by prayer and petition, with thanksgiving, present your requests to God."

Yep, that's what he said—don't be anxious. Just don't do it! No, it wasn't easy for him. Don't forget, his very life was at stake. That would cause anxiety in the best of us.

Yet the fact is, worry and indecision exact a huge toll on us. When we are worried or anxious, we cannot be emotionally balanced. Furthermore, those emotions don't accomplish one thing. No problem is ever solved by worry. No decision is ever made by worrying about it.

Sure, you will have decisions to make, sometimes extremely important ones. But instead of allowing yourself to worry, I suggest that you imagine your various options and mentally "try each one on." How does each look on you? How does it feel? Choose the one that gives you the most peace of mind. Once your choice has been made, stick to it. Refuse to allow yourself to wonder about any of the other options.

Suppose it isn't a decision that is causing you emotional imbalance. Suppose it is just general worry or anxiety that is haunting you. Here is a suggestion: Take out your Balance Journal and write down everything that is troubling you. Look at each item you have written down and ask yourself: "Is there anything I can do about this specific concern?" If the answer is "yes," vow to take constructive action. If the answer is "no," let go of it.

One of the best ways to beat anxiety is to look back at God's faithfulness to you in the past. If He has always met your needs before, can't you trust Him to meet them now?

So, identify the negative emotional habits in your life:

- disorganization
- not knowing your priorities
- worry
- indecision

Then work and pray toward eliminating them. Refuse to let them waste your valuable time or sap your energy any longer.

When you are able to turn the worry and anxiety over to God and let Him take it from you, "the peace of God, which transcends all understanding, will guard your hearts and your minds in Christ Jesus" (Phil 4:7).

The discipline of emotions is the training of responses.
—Elisabeth Elliot
Discipline: The Glad Surrender

Emotional Rest

We have talked about the importance of physical rest. Without it, our bodies cannot continue to function. Yet what about emotional rest? Just as physical rest gives our bodies a break from physical activity, emotional rest gives our minds respite from the wear and tear of anxiety, fear, tension, irritation, depression, unhappiness, and emotional fatigue.

What is emotional rest? It is peace, quiet, tranquility, contentment, and emotional refreshment. It means allowing our minds to rest from intellectual pursuits so that our emotions can also relax. It means the spiritual rest that comes with quiet time spent in God's presence.

To help you achieve spiritual rest, consider these emotional restoratives:

1. **Pause in your busy life to help others.** Volunteer your time at a soup kitchen, a hospital, or a shelter for the homeless, or delivering food to shut-ins via Meals on Wheels. It will help you to take your eyes off yourself and to see through the perspective of someone who has greater needs than you do.

2. **In your Balance Journal, keep a calendar of your emotions for a month or two.** This will help you to see what pulls you down and what brings you up.

3. **Make an ongoing list of things you're grateful for.** Don't forget the things most of us tend to take for granted—sight, a brain that works, a home in a free country, the right to worship God.

4. **Make a list of things that make you happy.** Keep it handy and add to it as other things come to mind.

5. **Refuse to feel sorry for yourself.** Don't let negative circumstances control you. Read books, watch videos, and listen to tapes about people who have overcome the most severe circumstances. You might want to start with Corrie ten Boom, author of the autobiography *The Hiding Place,* who spent years in a concentration camp, where she watched her family die, but who spent the rest of her life testifying to God's goodness and mercy. Or consider Joni Eareckson Tada, who, at the age of seventeen, broke her neck in a diving accident. Although destined to spend the rest of her life as a quadriplegic, she has ministered to millions all over the world through her art, music, writings, and speaking.

6. **Find a special place that refreshes and inspires you.** It might be a park bench, a mountain trail, a stretch of beach, a path in the woods, or even a corner of your own backyard. Use it as a regular retreat in which to read or reflect.

7. **Schedule a quiet time every day to meet with the Lord and pray.** Make this a priority and say "no" to anything that would interrupt you during that time. Let everyone know that unless there is a true emergency, no one is to disturb you during your quiet time.

8. **Seek out friends who build you up and bring out the best in you.** No, I don't mean friends who flatter you or say only what you want to hear. I mean those who encourage and inspire you to be the best you can be.

9. **Take a vacation from something.** Take a vacation from television, for instance, or from answering the telephone. In the interest of emotional balance, how about taking a vacation from complaining or criticizing?

10. **Close your eyes and picture your greatest achievement.** Is it owning your own home? Having a successful marriage after experiencing your parents' disastrous relationship? Building up a good business? Parenting great kids? Introducing someone to the Lord?

A Place of Solitude

Solitude is an important element in achieving emotional balance. As we have seen, some of us crave it more than others, but we all need it. Decide on a specific place that will be your place of solitude and a specific time when you will come before the Lord. Use your time to meditate, to pray, to seek God's guidance in making wise decisions in your life. Act on the promise of James 1:5: "If any of you lacks wisdom, he should ask of God, who gives generously to all without finding fault, and it will be given to him."

> Be still, and know that I am God.
>
> PSALM 46:10

Express Gratitude

Every day, make it a practice to find something for which to be thankful. Gratitude costs nothing and pays off so handsomely.

Last summer was a difficult one for me. My organization, Celebrate Life International, takes character and leadership training into public high schools. Summers always tend to be a tight time financially for us because school is out. Last summer was no exception. I was having a very, very difficult week with the finances—I had to lay off staff—and it was extremely hard to find a sense of joy and balance in the midst of all that pressure. Then, out of the blue, I got a telephone call.

"Zig Ziglar is on the line for you," my assistant told me.

I looked at her and said, "Yeah, right."

"No, he really is!" she said. "At least that's what the guy says. He told me he's Zig Ziglar."

I figured that one of my friends was playing a joke on me, because it was well known that Zig Ziglar was one of my role models. He is so good at demonstrating how to have a positive perspective, and how to live life according to your priorities. However, this was not a good day for a joke. Still, the light was flashing on my phone, so I thought, *Well, I'll just give whoever it is a piece of my mind.*

"Well, hello, Zig Ziglar!" I said enthusiastically. "How are you?"

And from the other end of the line came a voice, saying, "Hey, Lori. How are you?" As soon as I heard his greeting, I knew it really was he, because I've listened to so many of his tapes.

"Zig Ziglar!" I said. "I can't believe this is really you!"

"Lori," he said, "I want you to know that the other day, I heard about what you're trying to do in this country, how you're trying to impact the educational system of the United States of America with biblical truth and with gospel principles. And I got to thinking, that has to be heavy for you sometimes. So I decided to call you just to encourage you. Lori, you have a great vision and a great calling. No matter how difficult it becomes, always remember that if you can find the things you're thankful for, and if you can be grateful for all you have, and you can focus on that rather than on what you don't have, then that will get you through the heaviest times."

"Zig," I said, "I know that you and I have never met, but you have been such an encouragement to me."

"Well, you know what encouragement is?" he said. "It's putting courage into somebody's life. And one of the best ways that you can do that is to help them see the positive. Help them be grateful for the things they have, and then say to them, 'You can do this!'"

I was so encouraged after that phone call! How important it was to have someone remind me to be thankful for the things I have instead of focusing on what I don't have.

A good way to remind yourself to be grateful is to keep a

memory book or a list of things you can look to as your own Altars of Gratitude. (Your Balance Journal, of course, is a great place to start recording these.) When you look back at your Altars of Gratitude and remember how God provided for you in those circumstances, it will renew your faith that He can and will meet your needs today.

Yet there was another thing I got from that experience with Zig Ziglar. I realized that when God brings somebody to my mind, I need to be faithful to follow through with that person. Zig will never know how much fresh air that telephone call breathed into my weary soul. Breathing in the fresh air is very important. To achieve the balance, however, you need to breathe it out again. Receive and be revived, then give out again. A very important way to practice gratitude and to encourage one another is to help each other see the things for which we can be thankful.

Take some time to identify the things in your day that are God's way of reminding you that He is faithful and that He is in control. At the top of my list that day would have been a short telephone call.

God Is Faithful

Each of us is a gift from God, and each of us is a precious treasure. Here are some ways to protect and polish that treasure:

- surround yourself with positive people
- refuse to accept lies concerning yourself

- listen to positive, uplifting tapes
- read life-affirming books
- affirm what you know to be true about yourself
- make this affirmation out loud and with true conviction:
  "This is what I know to be true. My strengths are ___

  _____.

  My gifts and abilities are _____.
  I am good at doing these things: _____.
  This is how I contribute to the body of Christ: _____ .
  This is what I bring to the table at work: _____.
  This is what I add to my marriage: _____."

Such confidence as this is ours through Christ before God. Not that we are competent in ourselves to claim anything for ourselves, but our competency comes from God.

2 CORINTHIANS 3:4-5

It is way too easy to sabotage God's success in our lives by failing to allow ourselves to be all that God has created us to be.

We therefore need to affirm what we know to be true about ourselves. What is that? Well, in 2 Corinthians 3:18 we read, "And we, who with unveiled faces all reflect the Lord's glory, are being transformed into his likeness with ever-increasing glory, which comes from the Lord, who is the Spirit."

That's what we know, and that's what we need to affirm.

Develop Your Gifts

Again, build on your strengths and develop your gifts as thoroughly as you possibly can.

While there is nothing wrong with working on your weaknesses, keep in mind that instead of spending the majority of your time struggling to make those areas of your life passable, you could be strengthening your God-given gifts. He has given them to you, and He expects you to use them for the good of the body of Christ.

In my case, my strengths are that I am a visionary, I work well with people, and I am a good communicator. I am not a detail person, however, and administration is not a strong area for me. Now, I know that I have to learn how to balance my time, and I am learning to do so with my time systems notebook. It helps me make sure that I can keep my appointments, that I show up at the right places at the right times, and that I know what I am supposed to be doing. I have not, however, attempted to become a good administrator. Instead, I have surrounded myself with people who have the gift of administration, with people who are detail-oriented. Instead of putting a great deal of time and effort into working on strengthening that weakness, I maximize what I have by working within my strengths.

Make the most of what God has given you. I challenge you to run in the freedom of your strengths.

Never Give Up

The epitome of emotional balance is refusing to give up.

When I was a senior at Seattle Pacific University, I had to take a sociology class with all the freshmen. I have to tell you, I had an attitude when I entered that classroom. I mumbled, "Oh, brother! I can't believe I have to take this class with a lot of freshmen." It just seemed so beneath me.

We took our first test and I found it a little bit challenging, but I didn't think much of it. The next week when we came to class, the instructor had put the test scores up on the board, starting with the highest score and going on to the lowest. "Oh, man," I thought, "I really feel sorry for that person who got the lowest grade. Some dumb freshman who thought school was nothing but youth camp. Well, he'll learn."

You guessed it—that lowest grade was mine. I was so humiliated!

"Hey, Lori!" my friends were calling. "What did you get on your test?"

"Oh," I said, "I'd rather not say."

One of the girls said, "She probably got the highest grade in the class and doesn't want to brag."

A guy across the room said, "No, she didn't. I got the highest grade!"

Oh, great! I thought.

"So what *did* you get?" the guy asked.

"Well, I just don't want to say," I repeated, trying my best to sound humble and not as humiliated as I felt.

When Kurt came to pick me up that night, I was fit to be tied. "Kurt, I got the lowest grade in that whole class of freshmen. Can you believe this school? They obviously don't realize how lucky they are to have me as a student, or they wouldn't treat me this way. I mean, they gave me the lowest grade in the class! You know what, Kurt? I'm going to quit! I'm not going to take this kind of treatment! I'll do great things and validate my ministry, and I don't need them to do it!" I went on, and on, and on, and on, but the gist of all I said was, "I quit! I quit! I quit!"

I finally stopped, and we just walked in silence for a while. After a few minutes Kurt said, "So, I'm married to a quitter, am I?"

Wow! That didn't feel very good.

He shook his head and said, "I'm married to a quitter and I'm going to spend the rest of my life with a woman who couldn't handle a bad grade."

That did it. "If you think I'm going to quit over a small grade, you have another think coming!" I announced. "I'm not going to quit! I don't care how many bad grades I get, I'm not going to quit!" And on Monday morning I went back to that class with a completely different attitude.

Do not give up! Don't do it! Whether it's a grade or something far more devastating, the Lord Jesus Christ says, "I've given you My Spirit, and I will enable you to run the race. I will help you go the distance."

Hang in there. No matter how bad it gets, you must not give up.

You know what I want on my tombstone? *We couldn't keep her down.* I was slammed down? Boing! I was right back up. Down again? Boing! Down? Boing! Down really hard? Boing! No matter what happened, I kept on popping back up.

I will never, ever give up.

How about you?

Eight Pick-Me-Ups for a Cloudy Day

The best way to stay energized on a cloudy day is to know ahead of time what to do to stave off the letdown such a day can bring. What works for you? Here are some suggestions for you to try out:

1. Exercise, even if it's only a brisk twenty-minute walk.
2. Write down the top ten things you are thankful for today.
3. Read part of a book that lifts your spirits.
4. Recite the Scripture you have been memorizing.
5. Open your windows and let in as much light as possible.
6. Clean up your work environment.
7. Put a vase of flowers on your desk.
8. Play some favorite music.

Many people are so busy knocking themselves out trying to do everything they think they should do that they never get around to doing what they want to do. They never get to have fun. All work and no play may make your boss happy and keep your house clean, but it won't get you to a state of emotional balance.

Simplify Your Life

A wonderful way to move toward emotional balance is to get the clutter out of your life. Most of us have a junk drawer (many of us have a junk closet!). Every now and then it happens that we are frantically looking for something in there, but so much stuff has collected that we can't find anything. So, desperate and frustrated, we start throwing out all the unnecessary stuff, hoping that we will be able to find what we really care about.

Well, that just may be what you need to do with your life. You may need to take inventory and say, "What is all this stuff? Why am I filling up my time with junk and crowding out all the good stuff?" As you begin to sort, ask, "What can I eliminate so that I can get some order and balance in my life?"

That's what it means to simplify your life—simply to get rid of those things that are taxing you emotionally and are pulling you out of balance. Wherever you are going, you do not need to drag along any emotional baggage.

I think people are so preoccupied with material difficulties. In the industrial world where people are supposed to have so much, I find that many people, while dressed up, are really, really poor.

—Mother Teresa
Words to Love By

Emotional Buffers

Where can you find your own personal islands of emotional comfort? What is it that energizes and restores you? What is it that gives you

- more energy?
- a calmer day?
- a better attitude?
- the desire to go on and on?
- the determination to never give up?

Here are the answers some people gave to this question:

Tracy: "Warm water. I love to swim for energy and take a bubble bath to relax."

Suzanne: "Going outside. Whether it's biking, walking, or just sitting at the beach contemplating, being outside is both energizing and calming."

Rich:	"If I'm active, biking. If I'm quiet, crossword puzzles."
Tom and Lara:	"Pick-up basketball. We play it whenever we can. In the evenings, when we need to relax, we watch old musicals on television."
Walt:	"Gardening. There is nothing so restorative as getting down in the dirt and making something grow."

You say none of these appeals to you? No problem. Simply find what does. When you find what energizes you, what restores you, and what relaxes you, you are well on your way to achieving emotional balance.

Just for fun—well, not *just* for fun—here is an A to Z guide to emotional balance:

Accept yourself as you are.
Believe in yourself.
Consider the lilies.
Don't sweat the small stuff.
Envision the whole of you—even the unfinished parts.
Find humor in life.
Give unconditionally.
Help someone anonymously.
Influence a child for the good.
Join in on something fun.
Keep close to God.

Laugh out loud.

Meditate on a psalm.

Never give up on yourself.

Offer your gifts for the good of others.

Play restorative music.

Quit worrying.

Read books that encourage you.

Savor God's Word.

Think before you speak.

Understand the value of solitude.

Value yourself.

Whisper a prayer in the morning.

eXamine your priorities.

Yell when you need to.

Zap back to reality when you must.

Winston Churchill was invited back to the boys' school he had been kicked out of when he was a child. Now that he was famous, he had been invited to speak in an assembly before the whole school. He stepped up to the podium and, with his fist waving in the air, said, "Never, never, never, never, never, never, never, never, never give up." And then he sat down.

That's it! When you get struck down, you get back up. When you are knocked low, you get back up. When you're crushed, you pull yourself together and get back up. When you feel like you are being persecuted on every side, you endure the pain and get back up.

You may be hard-pressed on every side, but you will not

be crushed. It is impossible for you to be crushed. You may be perplexed, but you will not yield to despair. You cannot despair, because you've got the Lord living in you. You can be persecuted, but you will not be abandoned. You can be struck down, but you will not be destroyed.

Romans 8:37-39 assures us, "We are more than conquerors through Him who loved us. For I am convinced that neither death nor life, neither angels nor demons, neither the present nor the future, nor any powers, neither height nor depth, nor anything else in all creation, will be able to separate us from the love of God that is in Christ Jesus our Lord."

Wow!

Talk about emotional balance.

And it's all yours.

Balance Journal

Write down the words *Emotional Balance* and then explore these questions:

- What do I feel like now?

- What do I want to feel like?

- What could help me achieve more balance emotionally?

In the interest of emotional balance, you must:

- **Work on your attitude.**
  Start a list of things for which you are thankful. You can add to it whenever something comes to your mind. When you have filled one page, why not start a new journal just to be your thanksgiving journal?

- **Spend more time with your family.**
  Designate a certain meal when you will all eat together. Think of some things you can discuss around the table. How can you encourage sharing as well as listening?

- **Schedule fun time for yourself.**
  What might you do for the short term?
  What might you do for the long term?
- **Prevent blah days from getting you down.**
  Start a list of pick-me-ups you can do on short notice.

For immediate encouragement:

- List the ten things you've most enjoyed in the past week.
- … in the past month.
- … in the past year.
- … in your life.

Chapter 6

Finding Balance in Your Relationships

Remember your first-grade report card? It told your parents whether you were good or bad, smart or disappointing, promising or pathetic. It probably reported whether you tended to talk too much or too little, whether you played nicely or needed to learn to share, and whether you followed directions or did your own thing.

Before that first report card, most of us had no idea that the opinions of virtual strangers could affect and influence our parents' approval of us. In fact, those report cards may well have been the beginning of that difficult balance of relationships with which we all now have to deal. From those very earliest experiences some of us grew to believe that the most important relationship skill was to learn to please people. What an unfortunate lesson, for people-pleasing is neither godly nor healthy.

The goal of people-pleasing—or appeasing—is to make sure that people like us. Yet what actually happens is that the pleasers and appeasers usually end up feeling used, unappreciated, and driven to become all things to all people in order to maintain their image and to continue to receive approval. At first appearance, people-pleasers seem thoughtful and giving, but in fact they are slaves to the insatiable need to be admired, needed, and loved.

This results in relationships dangerously out of balance.

Family Relationships

Our first priority is to God, but our second is to our families. Family must come before job, hobby, friends, or, yes, even ministry.

> The Christian home is the Master's workshop where the processes of character molding are silently, lovingly, faithfully, and successfully carried on.
>
> —Richard Monckton Milnes

If you desire balance in your relationships, begin by establishing a home that is warm, hospitable, comfortable, and a haven of rest and peace to all who live there. All day long you, your spouse, and your children are with people who criticize you and tear you down, people who cause you anxiety and stress. Life just has a way of beating everyone up. Make your home just the opposite. Let it be a haven of peace, encouragement, love, and joy.

"That sounds great," I can almost hear you saying. "But you obviously don't know anything about my family life."

No, but if your family is like most today, you don't have

much time. Perhaps both you and your spouse work, or maybe you are a single parent who holds down two jobs just to make ends meet. Perhaps you live with your parents because you can't afford your own place, so you are scrimping and saving every dollar you can earn. Or maybe for the same reason, you are living with roommates, or are sharing a house with another family.

Whatever your situation, you are not alone. Juggling family, work, and living situations is a concern in most families.

Couples Together—Or Not

When families feel squeezed for time, very often it is the relationship between husband and wife that suffers the most. They know the importance of spending time together, but there just isn't any time for sharing romantic moments. "When our schedule is more free," they say, or "When the kids are older," or "When I catch up at work," or "When our grown kids get places of their own. Then there will be time for us." Yet that time comes—if it ever comes—so infrequently that many couples simply drift apart. By putting off shared romance, the two soon find that warmth and passion have disappeared from their relationship.

The sad fact is that many couples give their pets more time and attention than they do their own relationship. We'd never expect Felix or Fido to thrive without food and water, a good word, and a scratch behind the ears. Yet somehow we expect our marriages to grow and flourish without any time or attention at all.

"But what can I *do*?" you may be crying out in desperation. "I'm not just saying I'm too busy. I really *am* too busy!"

Good news! Romance doesn't have to be time-consuming. Look at the following suggestions and see how many you can put into practice with your own spouse. However, don't try these just once or twice. You may feel sort of awkward at first. Keep it up for a month or so and see if there isn't a warming trend between you.

- *Celebrate your daily homecomings.* What do you do for the first five minutes you are both home? Look at the mail? Listen to the answering machine? Mediate fights between the kids? Take the dog for a walk? Change that pattern. You see, the first five minutes you are together are crucial, because they set the tone for the rest of your evening. Leave the mail and the answering machine, send the kids to their rooms for just five minutes or have them walk the dog. Then focus exclusively on each other. Sit together on the sofa and tell each other about your day. Hug and kiss. Give each other a neck rub. Hold each other and just sit quietly. It's only five minutes, but those five minutes will remind you that you are a team working together toward a great goal—the success of your family.

- *Help your spouse help you.* One of the most destructive of emotions is resentment, the very one many spouses—especially wives—feel when it seems their partner isn't doing his or her share of the work. A 1993 Families and

Work Institute study found that men think they are doing more housework than they really are (43 percent of dual-income husbands said they were doing half the housework, while only 19 percent of dual-income wives felt that way). Interesting, isn't it? Yet to any individual, perception is reality. If you feel that your spouse isn't holding up his or her end, talk to him or her. Share your frustrations rather than allowing them to build up and wear on your relationship. Together make a list of the things each should be responsible for around the house and make an agreement that each will take care of his or her own responsibilities. Then let your spouse take responsibility. Don't jump in to pick up the slack.

- *Surprise one another.* Small surprises do a lot to put energy back into a relationship. Notes with expressions of love, relevant Scripture verses, or just an appropriate message ("I'll be praying for your meeting at 10:30") mean so much. Small gifts or flowers at unexpected times, cards that express a special sentiment, or even bringing home Chinese take-out on a busy day show you care.

- *Practice random acts of thoughtfulness.* Put out his vitamins in the morning. Set the VCR to record her favorite show. Pick up a magazine that features an article that will be of special interest to your spouse. Cut an appropriate and interesting article out of the paper.

   One couple we know is especially good at this. He makes her a cup of hot cocoa from scratch every morning and she takes the comics out of the newspaper and puts them in the bathroom for him! Those little actions might not mean much to anyone else, but to the two of them they demonstrate love.

- *Transform ordinary moments.* It's just an ordinary night after the kids are in bed and the dinner dishes are washed. Yet why not make it extraordinary by snuggling up in front of the television, holding hands like you used to, and toasting each other with a glass of sparkling cider? Or how about giving each other back-rubs? Or lighting a fire in the fireplace and reading to each other in the warm glow? It's just an ordinary night, but it can be transformed into something so special.

- *Plan date nights.* Most married couples have long since stopped dating. Big mistake! Once a week or once a month—whatever you can arrange—plan to get away together. And once you've set your date, don't break it except for the most serious of reasons.

"I know all those things," some of you may be saying. "I haven't done them yet, but I know them and I intend to start—sometime."

Good intentions are fine, but they don't go far enough. Focus on what you *actually* do rather than on what you *want* to do or what you *intend* to do. Do you come up short? Then do something about it now, before it's too late.

Relationships With Your Children

You have probably heard about the studies that show how little time families actually spend talking with one another. A 1994 Angus Reid poll, for instance, found that television watching was the main activity parents did with their children (an average of 6.3 hours per week). Other activities, such as reading to one another or helping with homework, received a mere 2.1 hours per week.

Of course, television allows you to just sit placidly and not *do* anything, an idea that sounds very appealing when you are tired after a long day at work. If you just wait for family interaction to happen, it may not—or at least not the way you want it to. Once again, you need to be proactive and *make it happen*. Here are some suggestions to help:

- *Go with routines.* You say your children don't like routine? Let me assure you, they will adapt. In fact, you will likely find that they even appreciate it. It gives them security by helping them know what to expect. If they know Saturday is laundry day, Sunday is church and then family day, Monday is grocery-shopping day, and so on, they won't be nearly so likely to badger and whine and complain about what they want to do. Discuss the routine with everyone, make the decision, then stick to it. By teaching your children how to schedule their day—get up at a certain time, feed the dog before school, do homework before dinner, watch one video or television show, go to bed at a set time—you will be teaching them a valuable lifelong skill.

- *Assign and post family jobs.* When family members know exactly what is expected of them, there are not nearly so many arguments and misunderstandings, and there is much more peace in the family. Write down each person's job assignments along with spaces to check off when the job is done. Post the list where everyone will see it (the refrigerator seems to be a favorite place). Then reward those who have all of their jobs checked off for an entire week (ice cream cones, popcorn, and extra time before bed are always popular rewards).

- *Don't expect perfection.* Not everything is going to be done perfectly. Accept and deal with it. If you don't, you will continue to fight a losing battle, and everyone—especially you!—will be worn to an emotional frazzle. Does it really matter if Jimmy's bed isn't made perfectly? Or if the laundry isn't folded exactly as you would do it? Your spouse may have a different way of mashing potatoes or making the bed, but does that really matter? Your children may not be that great at doing the vacuuming or dusting. So what? You will live longer—and a lot more happily—if you adopt a policy of "it's good enough" on those things that really don't matter. Save your stressing and nagging for the things that really do matter.

- *Consider outside help.* It's very difficult for some of us to get it through our heads, but some things are worth paying someone else to do. It just may be that the hourly wage you would pay someone to clean your house—or at least to do the heavy cleaning—would really be worth it when compared to the toll the time and stress take on you. Or what about the yard work? If it's something you hate and dread, think about hiring the boy next door. And what about that broken pipe in the bathroom that you have had on your to-do list for the last two months? Don't consider only the cost; also consider the emotional value of just getting it done.

- *Streamline your own schedule.* Instead of going grocery shopping on your way home from work every evening, save yourself a great deal of time and trouble by making a list and going shopping only once a week. If you can manage it, shopping at times and on days when there are fewer people in the stores will help you avoid those notorious long lines. When you run errands, group them together by area so you don't end up driving back and forth across town for something you forgot. Streamlining takes only a small amount of organization and planning, but the time and family stress you can save are considerable.

- *Set aside family time.* As with any relationship, it's important to plan time for your family to be together. Make time for regular family days—such as Sundays—when everybody sets aside together time. This doesn't have to be an entire day. Just a few hours would be great. You might go to church together, then have a picnic or play a game or fly kites or swing on swings. What you do isn't as important as the fact that you are spending the time together doing something that is enjoyable.

- *Trust your own decisions.* What if your boss asks you to work on Sunday? Or to put in overtime on the night of your child's piano recital? What if he or she insists that you spend a good deal of your time on the road? It's scary to say "no" to your boss, yet you resent having this intrusion into your family time. What do you do? Certainly I would never suggest that you take your job lightly. Yet if your priority is your family, you may need to speak up. Talk with your boss about your concerns. You may be happily surprised to find that he or she is pleased to work with you to discover a solution you both can accept. If not, you might want to start looking for another job, with a company that is more family-friendly.

- *Praise the efforts of others.* Everyone needs a pat on the back and a word of appreciation. When someone in the family does a job well, or does something extra just to help out, or makes any extra effort, be quick to praise and generous with your hugs and kisses. A smile or a thank-you encourages everyone to keep up the good work.

- *Reward yourselves.* Becoming a united family with a healthy relationship can be tough work. When you see positive steps, even little ones, congratulate and treat yourselves. Take the family out for ice cream. Go to a movie together. Take in a sporting event you all enjoy.

- *Don't allow outside interruptions.* The telephone rings while Junior is telling you about what happened at school today? Let it ring. Unexpected visitors stop by while you are helping your daughter with her science project? Tell them it's nice to see them but that you are busy at the moment. Don't be ashamed to let people know that your family time is a high priority to you.

- *Grab serendipitous moments.* That unplanned time you just happen upon can be the best relationship-building time of all: When you have just crawled in bed and your daughter peeks in and says, "Mom? Can I talk to you?" When your son is shooting baskets and he says, "Hey, Dad, how about a game of H-O-R-S-E?" When you have fifteen minutes to spare before you have to leave for work, just enough time to whip up some hot cocoa for you all to share. When your kids call out, "Look what's on TV!" and you pop a bowl of popcorn and sit down to watch with them. When the casserole is in the oven and the table is set, and you can sit on the floor and build with Legos with the kids for a few minutes. Don't let those minutes slip away. They are precious!

Divert, Withdraw, Abandon

Balance, in relationships as in other areas of our lives, requires rest and relaxation. Without it, we cannot go the distance. I really like Rick Warren's formula for lasting. He says:

- Divert daily
- Withdraw weekly
- Abandon annually

What does this mean, practically speaking? Well, to *divert daily* means to take a little "vacation" every day. This could be getting a Venti Mocha at Starbucks, taking time to read the newspaper, enjoying a hot bath with candles burning and music playing, or grabbing a twenty-minute nap while your toddler is sleeping.

To *withdraw weekly* means to take at least one day off each week. You might partner with other parents and take their kids for a day, then allow them to reciprocate by taking yours. It may mean going off with your spouse, or it may mean going off for some time alone. Depending on what you enjoy, this could be anything from a game of golf to a day of shopping to breakfast with friends to a visit to the art museum.

To *abandon annually* means to take a yearly vacation. It may mean traveling somewhere, or it may mean going camping close by, or it may mean staying home but not answering the telephone or the door. In almost every community there are things to do and see and enjoy that residents never get around to pursuing.

Divert daily, withdraw weekly, abandon annually. It really makes a lot of sense, doesn't it? If you are rested and refreshed, getting your relationships in balance will be much easier.

A happy family is but an earlier heaven.

—Sir John Bowring

Friendships in Balance

We all need friends, even the most private of us. We need one another's encouragement, mentoring, and love. We need to be accountable to one another. And we need to know we matter to people outside our own family.

"Snowflakes are fragile," the saying goes, "but if enough of them stick together they will stop traffic." It's true for snowflakes, and it's true for people. If you have friends who will stick with you through thick and thin, you can withstand the disappointments, difficulties, and unfairness of life.

We need to have friends, and we need to be friends.

God evidently does not intend us all to be rich, or powerful or great, but He does intend us all to be friends.

—Ralph Waldo Emerson

Positive Versus Negative

I can't choose those to whom I minister, but I can choose with whom I hang out. Part of finding balance in our lives is finding out which relationships are truly beneficial and which merely clutter up our lives. It sounds harsh, but it is reality. Are there some relationships in your life that simply need to go?

> The perfect friendship is that between good men alike in their virtue.
>
> —Aristotle

You have the right to say "no" to maintaining friendships with people who rob you of your balance. Negative people are balance-robbers. You will do well to avoid them. You say your colleagues spend lunchtime every day sitting around in the employee lunchroom, complaining about their lives, and you always feel worse for having been with them? Then don't be with them. Take a walk at lunchtime. Run some errands that will save you time after work. Sit alone and read. Put on earphones and listen to music.

You say your friends at the athletic club spend their time criticizing the dirty rotten politicians that are destroying this country? You say that they constantly complain that everyone gets a break but them? Then do your aerobics class or play your game of racquetball and leave. Don't sit around with them and allow them to make you unhappy and dissatisfied.

You say the neighborhood friend with whom you walk each morning spends the entire time complaining about her crummy marriage and her ungrateful kids? Then don't walk with her. Walk by yourself in the evening or find someone else with whom to walk.

Life is too short to be constantly pulled down. Seek out friends who inspire you and encourage you to be the best you can be.

Also watch out for the "Beleaguered Buddies." These are the "friends" who never get around to committing to their own goals. Instead, they pull you into their procrastination with them. They stop by your home or office to complain about their nasty bosses or their awful spouses or the churches they won't go to because they are full of hypocrites. If anyone suggests that they just might be able to improve their lives, their attitude becomes one of helplessness: "You just don't know how hard I've tried!" or "Nothing ever works out for me. If anything can possibly go wrong, it will!" or "No one will ever give me a break."

Beleaguered Buddies are extremely high-maintenance relationships. They will cause you to waste many valuable hours of your time, and they will sap you of emotional strength.

You may have experienced this. "Everyone thinks she is such a good person," you say. "I know I should be her friend, but it is just wearying for me to be with her."

Everyone may be right. Maybe this acquaintance is a good person. Maybe she is a good friend for everyone else—but not for you. Listen to others, but trust yourself. If a person is a drain on you, for whatever reason, don't get entangled in a relationship with that person. Relational balance requires that you eliminate relationships that clutter your life or pull you down. Instead, nurture the relationships that bring peace, harmony, and balance into your life.

> Friendship is unnecessary, like philosophy, like art....
> It has no survival value; rather it is one of those things
> that gives value to survival.
>
> —C.S. Lewis
> *The Four Loves*

Flowers for the Living

Sometimes I'll be out with some girlfriends—maybe hiking in the clean outside air, or maybe lunching at a favorite hole in the wall—and I'll say, "You know what, you guys? This is a sacred moment. Right now, right here, we are having a sacred moment together."

It's true. I believe it with all my heart. In eternity, we may well be able to look back over our lives and see that moments such as this truly did bring a blessing to us.

I was once in Venezuela with a group of twelve or thirteen people, and we were climbing way up in the Andes Mountains. We looked out on the beauty of the mountain range and the clouds and all the greenery. It was so beautiful that it silenced us all. None of us could say a word because the beauty was so breathtaking. After a few moments of silence, one by one, people began to weep. Still, not a word was spoken. There was no music, no altar call, no speaker. There was nothing but the sound of God's creation, yet it spoke to us in such a profound way that tears rolled down our faces.

After those moments of silence and weeping we looked at one another and realized that we had experienced a pristine time of worship. For the longest time, no one dared to speak a word. Yet after many more moments of silence and tears, we gathered together, and one girl—a new Christian—looked at me and said, "Lori, what is this? What's happening here?"

"It's a sacred moment," I said. "It's a holy moment. It's a moment where we worship simply because we are aware of God's presence. He visited us in a moment that we don't ever want to forget. We want to be able to return to this moment again and again."

The power of memories can bring us a great deal of balance. When we are in the midst of a hectic moment or a discouraging circumstance, when we are ill or sad, when our friends have let us down and everything seems wrong, we can go back to that moment and regain our balance. I can go back to Venezuela, back to the Andes Mountains, back to that moment when nothing was done or spoken. I can go back in my memory to the time when God visited me.

Where have you experienced sacred moments, and with whom? It is important to recognize them.

Yet it is difficult to have sacred moments if we allow things and people to crowd out all the sacred spaces in our lives. Sacred moments, when God's Spirit visits us and brings well-being to our souls, happen when we create sacred space in our lives. So protect that sacred space. Refuse to allow anything or anyone to crowd it out.

I am so big on sacred moments that some of my friends tease me and say, "Lori, is this a sacred moment?"

I don't mind. It's important to me to verbally remind people to acknowledge these times in our lives.

Just as our sacred moments will pass unnoticed if we aren't attuned to them, so will the goodness and love of friends pass unnoticed if we fail to acknowledge it. If we are going to achieve relational balance, it is vital that we slow down the pace of our lives and pause to give people the flowers due them while they are still around to enjoy the fragrance.

My mom used to tell us kids, "You know, people always wait to give folks their flowers after they are dead. They bring them to the funeral and lay them before the casket. But the people can't smell them then. They can't see and enjoy them after they are gone."

This doesn't mean you need to actually hand each person a bouquet, of course. No, the way to give people flowers while they are living is to come up with something positive about each person's character or personality and then give that person his or her "flowers" by speaking a thoughtful word, sending a note, or making a telephone call. It doesn't have to cost a thing, yet it can mean so much.

To whom would you like to give a special "flower"? Why not set aside time today to make a call or write a note?

Relational Rest

When you have your relationships in balance, you will experience a special thing called relational rest. This simply means that you will have a sense of peace and harmony with other people. Just imagine! Peace and harmony in your home, in your church, in your school, in your workplace—indeed, throughout your community.

Relationships of peace and harmony don't come about unless you have a heart of love and a soul that is at peace with God. As a matter of fact, your spiritual, physical, mental, and emotional rest are all deepened and brought into balance when you receive the gifts of the Spirit offered through Christ Jesus.

But the fruit of the Spirit is love, joy, peace, patience, kindness, goodness, faithfulness, gentleness and self-control. Against such things there is no law.... Since we live by the Spirit, let us keep in step with the Spirit.

GALATIANS 5:22-23, 25

We all need fellowship, and we need deep friendships—ones that are steeped in prayer, free for vulnerable sharing, and filled with forgiveness. We all need friends who encourage balance in our lives.

Balance Journal

In the section *Balance in Your Relationships*, take some time to weigh your own family relationships.

How are you encouraging balance in your family?

- Your family may include your spouse, your children, your parents, your siblings, your parents-in-law, your roommates, or whoever else has a regular family interaction with you.

Describe the balance of relationships with

- Your friends
- Your coworkers
- Your neighbors
- People at church
- Others

Make a list of the fruits of the Spirit from Galatians 5:22-23.

- Which ones do you see flourishing in your life?
- Which ones do you need to nurture?
- Are there any that seem to be nonexistent?
- Are there special people who encourage the fruits to flourish in your life?
- How might you give "flowers" to those people while they are still living?

Chapter 7

A Celebration of Balance

In going through this book with me you have done a great deal to bring balance to your life in these pivotal areas:

- spiritually
- physically
- mentally
- emotionally
- relationally

Good work! Now you have one more thing to do: Celebrate!

Certainly you should celebrate your accomplishments, goals, and decisions, but don't stop there. If your life is to be truly balanced, put on the crowning touch by determining that for you celebration will be a regular part of it. Celebrate frequently and celebrate well. Good and frequent celebrations will bring a sense of joy to your life.

You say you do celebrate? You say Christmas and Thanksgiving are big times for you? That you never miss a birthday or a graduation? That you even make a big deal out of anniversaries and Valentine's Day?

That's great. However, I'm not talking simply about the big times in your life. I'm talking *frequency*. Even when there isn't a big reason. Even when there isn't time for a real bash or money for nonessentials. Actively watch for small reasons to celebrate, and when you find them, snatch them up. You'll discover that they will bring a new sense of joy to your existence and a more complete balance to your life. For celebrations that happen in the small moments of life bring a sense of relief and joy to a heavy and hectic life and world like nothing else can.

When I was a student at Fuller Theological Seminary, I worked long, hard hours. One year, during finals week, the workload was especially heavy. My classmates and I were learning Hebrew and Greek, and we had theology classes that were especially difficult. One of the girls we hung out with was from England. I remember walking out of class one day, every one of us burdened down with books to read and homework to do. There just were not enough hours in the day and night to do it all. We didn't even have enough energy to complain, so we just walked along together in silence.

Suddenly the girl from England announced, "Tomorrow afternoon at two o'clock I want you all to come to my house."

I looked at her as if she was out of her mind. "What are you talking about?" I exclaimed. "I don't have time to come to your house!"

"I don't have time, either," each of the other girls chimed in.

"All I'm asking for is three-quarters of an hour," our friend said. "I want you all to meet at my house for just forty-five minutes. That's all."

Although not a one of us felt we had forty-five minutes to give, we all grudgingly agreed to meet her. It was, after all, less than an hour, and we did want to be kind to her. So we all showed up at the appointed hour, and there, in her front yard, in the glorious Pasadena, California, sunshine, she had a lovely table all set up. It was just a picnic table, but it was covered with a pretty tablecloth and there were candles and flowers in the center. On the table were teacups and a matching teapot, and there was a plate of delicious-looking scones. Right there, in the middle of a hectic finals week, we had an honest-to-goodness English tea party.

For forty-five minutes, all of us girls sat around that little picnic table. What a relief it was to set aside our worries and labors and share such fun and laughter. What a gift to have that small, unexpected island of diversion in the middle of such a hectic schedule.

In England, our friend told us, they considered it most important to take time out of the day and drink tea. Yet when the forty-five minutes were over, she said a prompt good-bye, and we all left, renewed, restored, and truly thankful.

When I look back on my seminary education, that impromptu tea party is one of the moments I will never forget. That day, sitting in the sunshine around that lovely picnic table, I learned the importance of celebration. To this day, in my marriage, in my relationships, at work, in every area of my life, I make it a point to stop at unlikely moments and celebrate. I want to do it frequently and I want to do it well.

Moments of seeing beauty are the pinnacles of our experience, lifting us out of the dreary circumstances and giving us pleasure and delight until we fall back and again become our ordinary selves. They must be interwoven into our daily existence in order to make life endurable and sweet. If we do not train ourselves to receive beauty when it appears before us our memory bank will be filled with only the products of the mind, the will, the intellect—cold, logical, and calculating—without serenity, heart, humor, or warmth.

—Luci Swindoll
You Bring the Confetti, God Brings the Joy

One thing that makes it possible to celebrate frequently and at impromptu moments is to have things already in place, just waiting for an occasion to celebrate. One thing I do is buy nonalcoholic sparkling cider whenever I find it on sale. I always have a bottle of it in my car and another in my refrigerator, because I so love spontaneous celebrations that I want to be ready for them. If someone comes home with an "A," if good news comes in the mail, if something goes well at work—even if there is a very simple reason, such as the garden doing well—we can pop open a bottle and celebrate.

What are some things you might have ready for a celebration? It all depends, I know. So it's best to have things on hand to allow you to celebrate events with the various people in your life: your spouse, your children, your friends, your coworkers, your visiting guests. Your list might be different than mine, but here are some suggestions:

- candles
- colored paper streamers
- confetti
- balloons
- party stickers
- brightly colored napkins
- ice cream and cones
- a favorite frozen dessert
- a frozen pizza
- bottled bubbles for blowing
- handmade coupons for favorite treat spots such as an ice cream shop, a movie theater, the garden center, a video rental store

I know one family whose "spontaneous celebration" collection fills an entire hallway cabinet and contains a selection of small, inexpensive gifts such as note cards, stickers, and small treats. "We buy things after the season, when they are half-price. A small Valentine stuffed animal, for instance, can say, 'I love you,' any time of the year. After Easter jelly beans are always a treat. A mug specifically aimed for 'Daddy' or 'my dear sister' can be just the right thing. Anyway, who says we can't have a little bit of Christmas in the middle of July?"

Celebrate Your Gifts

God calls us to do great things, and best of all, He gives us the ability to do them. When we seek His will, and desire above all else to follow His plan and His commandments, then our ambitions and goals are pleasing to Him. When we are pleasing Him, He takes pleasure in our celebration. Do you doubt this? Consider these verses:

Then all the people went away to eat and drink, to send portions of food and to celebrate with great joy, because they now understood the words that had been made known to them.

NEHEMIAH 8:12

They will celebrate your abundant goodness
and joyfully sing of your righteousness.

PSALM 145:7

You will sing as on the night you celebrate a holy festival; your hearts will rejoice as when people go up with flutes to the mountains of the Lord, to the Rock of Israel.

ISAIAH 30:29

"My son," the father said, "you are always with me, and everything I have is yours. But we had to celebrate and be glad, because this brother of yours was dead and is alive again; he was lost and is found."

LUKE 16:31-32

Do you want a good reason to celebrate? Just look at these:

- Remember what God has done!
- Remember where you are headed!
- Remember who you are!

Yesterday, Today, Someday

Yesterday you likely celebrated less than you now wish you had. Today you are trying to make celebration a greater part of your life. Someday ... ah, someday. Someday you will do the wonderful things of your dreams. Someday you will see the pyramids of Egypt. Someday you will write the story of your family. Someday you will visit Rome and Paris and London. Someday you will run a marathon race. Someday you will bike across your state. Someday ...

Do you know what your "somedays" are? They are your dreams and goals. Of course, some are more dreams and others are more goals. Which of the two are your somedays? Here is an easy way to help you determine: Ask yourself, "If money were no object, and I had no obligation to anyone, would I jump out of bed tomorrow morning and be on my way to do that 'someday'?" If you would, it is likely a true goal. However, if you would crawl back in bed and say, "Maybe some other time," then it is probably just a dream.

Someday Folder

If a someday is a dream, go ahead and enjoy dreaming, but realize that's all it is. If your dream is a goal, however, begin now to bring it to reality. Start by making it as tangible as possible. A good way to do this is to put together a "someday folder." Collect things that will demonstrate your someday goals. For instance, if your goal is to build a sailboat, begin to collect building plans. If your goal is to make your backyard into an English garden, start gathering pictures of English gardens that appeal to you. If your goal is to make a handmade quilt, begin to collect quilt blocks and pictures of quilts that strike your fancy.

A someday folder is more than just a collection of wishes and whimsies. It is a hands-on plan for what will very possibly one day be.

Far away in the sunshine are my highest aspirations.
I may not reach them,
but I can look up and see their beauty,
believe in them,
and try to follow where they lead.

—Louisa May Alcott

One of my somedays that I have already accomplished is going to India to see Mother Teresa's work in action. (In fact, I have been there five times so far.) The sisters there seem to have such a sense of peace and well-being in the midst of incredible circumstances and a schedule that is unbelievably challenging. The first time I was in Calcutta, one of the most impressive things to me was the sisters' prayer time. They pray before they do anything. For them, prayer is truly a key thing. It meant so much to me because prayer is such a key part of my life, too.

To be perfectly honest, though, it also almost irritated me. The sisters had such an incredible sense of being centered. They actually seemed to be at peace right down to their inner core. So I went up to one of the sisters and asked, "How do you all get this way?" I mean, we were standing in the middle of unbelievable poverty and sickness and disease and death. People were literally dying on the doorsteps. They had hundreds of kids there, as well as hundreds of leprosy patients. There were sick and homeless people everywhere. And yet, in the midst of it all, these sisters had an almost palpable sense of peace.

"How do you do it?" I asked, looking around me. "How in the world do you all do this?"

That humble woman looked at me, smiled, and said, "Lori, Lori. You're worried and bothered about so many things. It's really very simple. We pray and we obey. It's moment-by-moment surrender."

"I know that," I said a bit impatiently. "But what I mean is, how do you achieve that peaceful disposition?"

"Lori," she said, "if you did what I just said, you would not be asking me this question. It is moment-by-moment surrender. It is praying and letting God bring the idea to your mind. Then it is doing what God tells you to do."

I came away from the experience finally realizing the truth of what that sister had told me. It truly is moment-by-moment. That peace really is a matter of surrendering each and every moment in whatever we do. Are you feeding your baby or changing a diaper? Are you meeting an impossible deadline at work? Are you commuting in rush-hour traffic? Are you enduring an unbelievably difficult person? Are you fixing your leaking plumbing, or mowing the lawn, or washing the laundry, or picking up toys off the floor? These can be moments of worship for you. Because for a child of God, everything you do—*every single thing*—is to be done as unto God. That is the way these sisters brought such a wonderful sense of balance to their existence. That is what led to such great peace under the most unpeaceful of circumstances.

Even in the immediate hectic-ness of life—yes, even *your* life—we can have that moment-by-moment surrender to the Lord. We can pray to Him anywhere and under any circumstance. We can surrender whatever He brings into our minds. That obedience will bring about a sense of balance, and that balance will lead us to joyful celebration.

Lord Christ
Your Servant
Martin Luther
said he only had
two days
on his calendar:
today
and "that day."
And that's
what I want too.
And I want
to live
today
for
that day.

—Joseph Bayly

Growing Older Joyfully

Our society puts a great deal of emphasis on youth. Look young, we are told. Act young. If you allow yourself to grow old, you are no longer of value. I beg to differ. Growing older is a natural part of life. Ideally, growing older also means grow-ing in wisdom and maturity. Shouldn't that make it something to be desired?

When we are young and inexperienced, we look for role

models and mentors. One of my personal mentors is writer-speaker Luci Swindoll. She has been especially important in my life, because she has been a special kind of mentor—a joy mentor. Here is what she has to say about growing older:

> Growing older can be unbelievably exciting. It can truly be a joyful experience as we look for new paths of broadening our minds, enlarging our horizons, loving different people and new things, reaching across prejudicial barriers. Simply put, it takes getting outside ourselves and creating what is not, balanced and blended with getting inside ourselves and accepting what is.

All my life, I have been involved in a special "prayer and share" time with my family. Kurt and I have carried on this tradition in our own marriage. As we grow older, it has become an even more precious part of my life. "Prayer and share" takes place at the end of the day. Each person gives one prayer request and one highlight of the day. It gives us a chance to reflect on the ways in which the Lord has worked in each of our lives during the day.

This is a great thing to do as a family, but it is also something you can do alone. Before you go to bed, ask yourself:

- *What has God done for me today?*
- *What has He done through me today?*
- *What is my prayer request for tonight?*

This kind of reflection will give a whole new meaning to your day. What better way to lead you to celebration? God got your attention through something. He spoke to you through particular events of your life. He showed you once again the importance of communing with Him. Once again He drew you into praise of Him. God was truly at work.

Wow!

Be joyful!

Celebrate!

On the Threshold of Tomorrow

Although you rejoice and celebrate today, tomorrow will be even better. You have learned new things and you have been introduced to new experiences. Tomorrow you will encounter:

- increased opportunities
- increased experiences
- increased ministry
- increased wisdom
- increased satisfaction
- increased peace
- increased joy
- increased celebration

How you react to today is the key to what you will experience tomorrow. You don't know what is coming in your future. None of us does. Yet what actually happens is not what will determine who and what we will be. Two people can experience exactly the same circumstance, and one will be devastated while the other is encouraged and strengthened.

> *Two men looked through prison bars;*
> *one saw the mud, the other saw the stars.*

Look past your problem, and you will see God's purpose. Guess what? God's purpose is always greater than the problem. That's the truth that will enable you to go the distance.

> We have an idea that God is leading us to a particular end, a desired goal; He is not. The question of getting to a particular end is a mere incident. What we call the process, God calls the end.... His purpose is that I depend on Him and on His power now. If I can stay in the middle of the turmoil calm and unperplexed, that is the end of the purpose of God.... His end is the process.... It is the process, not the end, which is glorifying to God.
>
> —Oswald Chambers
> *My Utmost for His Highest*

Dear Christian, you are on your mark!
Get set!
Go!

Run the race, and run it to the finish line. Your greatest celebration of all is still to come. It will occur on that blessed day when the Lord says to you, "My good and faithful servant, I am pleased with your race."

Balance Journal

In this final section entitled *Celebrate!* you can begin your own "prayer and share" time.

List the significant things that have happened to you today.

- How did God try to get your attention?
- What did you learn from this?
- Reflect upon the meaning of your day.
- For what can you praise God today?
- How can you celebrate?